C0-AVT-013

THE BOOK
of
COMMON ORDER
of
THE UNITED CHURCH OF CANADA

AUTHORIZED BY
THE GENERAL COUNCIL

TORONTO
THE UNITED CHURCH PUBLISHING HOUSE

ACKNOWLEDGEMENTS

Free use has been made of the *Ritual* of the Methodist Church (Canada) and of the *Book of Common Order* of the Presbyterian Church in Canada (1922).

Grateful acknowledgement is made of indebtedness to the service books of the ancient and mediaeval Church, those of the Anglican and Lutheran Communions, and those of Scottish and American Churches.

If any copyright has been infringed, the Committee hopes that the oversight may be forgiven.

Second Edition (revised and reset), 1950.

PREFACE

IN the Churches which united to form The United Church of Canada there was an ordered liberty in common worship. They followed lines marked out by Apostolic practice and hallowed by the general usage of Christendom, but they shrank from a uniformity that might quench the Spirit of God in the soul of man. In our worship we are rightly concerned for two things: first, that a worshipping congregation of the Lord's people shall be free to follow the leading of the Spirit of Christ in their midst; and secondly, that the experience of many ages of devotion shall not be lost, but preserved, —experience that has caused certain forms of prayer to glow with light and power.

This book has been prepared by the Committee on Church Worship and Ritual of The United Church of Canada. The aim of the Committee has been to set forth orders that are loyal to the Spirit of Christ and loyal to the experience of the Church of all ages and of all lands; orders that carry on the devotional usage of the three uniting Communions in their living integrity. It is hoped that they may prove fit to be regarded as normative, and also be found flexible enough for the many-sided life of a growing Church.

The Committee prays that those who use this book may be enabled by it to enter more fully into the rich heritage of Christian worship,—and find that the good Shepherd has there provided for his flock "green pastures" and "waters of comfort."

SOLI DEO GLORIA

NOTES ON SOME OF THE ORDERS

1. Public Worship

THE First Directory has the structure of Morning and Evening Prayer. The central elements were: (1) the meditative recitation of the Psalms as an act of praise; (2) the reading of Lessons from Holy Scripture. The Prayers at first stood mainly at the beginning; the Sermon in time found a place at the end.

The Hymnary (before No. 692) contains directions in regard to the use of the Psalms.

The Second Directory has the structure of the Lord's Supper. The main elements are: (1) The Word of God read and preached (Lessons and Sermon): (2) the Fellowship of intense and intimate Prayer.

Each Directory is followed by two Orders of the same structure as the Directory.

There is also a Directory for an Evening Service.

The Directories are followed by a selection of Prayers to be used with them: (1) a collection of *Prayers and Thanksgivings,* out of which what is needed for a General Prayer may be taken; (2) a *Treasury* of (Occasional) Prayers.

2. The Table of Lessons

The Lord's people should hear the great passages of Scripture at least once a year. The *Table of Lessons* has therefore been confined largely to those central passages that gather closely about: (1) Christ's work of Redemption (Advent to Pentecost, half the year), and (2) the application of that work to believers (Pentecost to Advent, the other half of the year). The Lessons are set down in groups of two or three; with each group there stands a Prayer for Grace cognate in thought and intention.

3. The Lord's Supper

This rite has from the beginning included two movements: (1) the reading and preaching of the Word of God; and (2) the re-enactment of what took place in the Upper Room when our Lord sat at meat with his disciples for the last time. Introductory movements grew up in the Church in great variety, and took their place before the reading of Scripture; these have always been subsidiary to the two principal movements.

The Church has always been careful to make the second movement follow (in four stages) the four verbs of the Gospel narrative: "Jesus *took* bread, . . . *gave thanks,* . . . *brake,* . . . *gave* to them." The "Breaking" may stand alone, or be joined with the Prayer (gave thanks), or with the Delivery (gave).

The two Orders set down here have the same structure; but in the second the Introduction and the whole of the first movement are summed up in a single rubric.

4. Baptism

The core of the rite is the use of water with the words: "N. I baptize thee, etc." To bring out the full meaning there is prefixed instruction passing into personal questions; and the whole action unfolds in an atmosphere of prayer.

5. Ordination

This order was adopted by the General Council held at Winnipeg in 1928 as "The Order for Ordination in The United Church of Canada."

6. Women Missionaries and Deaconesses

These two are often used at the same time; they appear here as a double Order. It will probably be easier for a Presiding Minister when one Order only is required to leave out what he does not need, than to piece together two distinct Orders when they are wanted together.

CONTENTS

CONTENTS

THE FIRST DIRECTORY FOR

THE PUBLIC WORSHIP OF GOD

THE INTRODUCTION

¶ *The Minister shall call the People to worship, saying,* Let us worship God, *or words to the same effect, or he may use fitting words taken from Holy Scripture; and then he shall lead the People in a Prayer of Invocation; then shall a Psalm or Hymn be sung; then shall the Minister lead the People in Prayers of Confession and of Supplication; after which, where it is customary, they may say together the Lord's Prayer.*

¶ *Or else, the Service shall begin with a Psalm or Hymn of approach to the God of all grace; and then the Minister shall lead the People in Prayers of Invocation, of Confession, and of Supplication; after which, where it is customary, Minister and People may say together the Lord's Prayer.*

THE PSALMS

¶ *Then shall one or more Psalms be sung or said, with this Conclusion,*

Glory be to the Father, and to the Son: and to the Holy Ghost; As it was in the beginning, is now, and ever shall be: world without end. Amen.

THE LESSONS

¶ *Then shall a Lesson be read, taken out of the Old Testament.*

¶ *After which a Canticle or a Psalm or a Hymn may be sung.*

¶ *Then shall a second Lesson be read, taken out of the New Testament.*

¶ *Or else, the first Lesson shall be taken out of an Epistle, or the book of Acts, or the Revelation of St. John, and the second out of a Gospel.*

¶ *Or else, one Lesson only shall be read, taken out of the New Testament.*

¶ *Before the first Lesson is read the Minister shall say,* Let us hear the Word of God, as it is contained in such a book, such a chapter, beginning at such a verse; *and likewise at the beginning of the second Lesson; and after the latter,* The Lord bless to us the reading of his Holy Word, and to his name be glory and praise.

¶ *Or else, he shall say before every Lesson,* Here beginneth such a chapter, *or* such a verse of such a chapter, of such a book, *and after every Lesson,* Here endeth the first, *or* the second Lesson, *or* the Lesson.

THE PRAYERS

¶ *Then shall follow Prayer, the Minister in the name of all, giving praise and thanks to God for all his benefits, and above all for his inestimable love in the redemption of the world by our Saviour Jesus Christ; entreating God of his grace to receive the offering which we now make of ourselves, in union with him who loved us and gave himself for us; making intercession with the Father of mercies for the Church, for the Nation, and for the whole family of Mankind, and for all sorts and conditions of men; and remembering with thankgiving the whole company of the faithful dead who are now at one with him, especially those dear to our own hearts. And then, if it hath not been said already, Minister and People shall say together the Lord's Prayer.*

¶ *Then shall the Offerings of the People be collected and presented; and, if it be desired, a suitable Anthem may be sung. Or else, the Offerings may be received after the Sermon.*

THE SERMON

¶ *Then shall a Hymn be sung; before or after which such Announcements as are needful and fitting shall be made.*

¶ *Then shall follow the Sermon, the Minister taking his text from the Word of God, and remembering that it is his office to instruct the People in divine truth, to set forth Christ crucified as their Saviour, and to incite them to Christian faith and duty.*

¶ *Then shall follow thanksgiving for the Word of God, prayer for perseverance in the divine grace, with remembrance of the whole Church of Christ.*

¶ *Then shall a Psalm or Hymn be sung.*

¶ *And the Minister shall let the People depart with the Blessing.*

AN ORDER FOR

THE PUBLIC WORSHIP OF GOD

ACCORDING TO THE FOREGOING DIRECTORY

THE INTRODUCTION

¶ *The Minister shall call the People to worship, saying,* Let us worship God, *or words to the same effect, or he may use fitting words taken from the Holy Scripture. Then shall he say,*

Let us pray.

ALMIGHTY and everlasting God, who art always more ready to hear than we to pray, and art wont to give more than either we desire, or deserve: Pour down upon us the abundance of thy mercy; forgiving us those things whereof our conscience is afraid, and giving us those good things which we are not worthy to ask, but through the merits and mediation of Jesus Christ, thy Son, our Lord. *Amen.*

¶ *Then shall a Psalm or Hymn be sung.*

¶ *Then shall follow this Confession and Prayer for Pardon.*

ALMIGHTY and most merciful Father; We have erred and strayed from thy ways like lost sheep. We have followed too much the devices and desires of our own hearts. We have offended against thy holy laws. We have left undone those things which we ought to have done; And we have done those things which we ought not to have done; And there is no health in us. But thou, O

Lord, have mercy upon us, miserable offenders. Spare thou them, O God, which confess their faults. Restore thou them that are penitent; According to thy promises declared unto mankind in Christ Jesus our Lord. And grant, O most merciful Father, for his sake; That we may hereafter live a godly, righteous, and sober life, To the glory of thy holy name. Amen.

O GOD, whose nature and property is ever to have mercy and to forgive: Receive our humble petitions; and though we be tied and bound with the chain of our sins, yet let the pitifulness of thy great mercy loose us; for the honour of Jesus Christ, our Mediator and Advocate. *Amen.*

¶ *Then shall follow this, or other Prayer for Grace contained in this book.*

O GOD, the protector of all that trust in thee, without whom nothing is strong, nothing is holy: Increase and multiply upon us thy mercy; that, thou being our ruler and guide, we may so pass through things temporal, that we finally lose not the things eternal: Grant this, O heavenly Father, for Jesus Christ's sake our Lord. *Amen.*

¶ *After which, where it is customary, the Lord's Prayer may be said by Minister and People together.*

OUR Father, who art in heaven, Hallowed be thy name; Thy kingdom come; Thy will be done; In earth as it is in heaven. Give us this day our daily bread. And forgive us our trespasses, As we forgive them that trespass against us. And lead us not into temptation; But deliver us from evil: For thine is the kingdom, The power, and the glory, For ever and ever. Amen.

THE PSALMS

¶ *Then shall one or more Psalms be sung or said, with this Conclusion,*

Glory be to the Father, and to the Son: and to the Holy Ghost; As it was in the beginning, is now, and ever shall be: world without end. Amen.

THE LESSONS

¶ *Then shall a Lesson be read, taken out of the Old Testament.*

¶ *After which a Canticle or a Psalm or a Hymn may be sung.*

¶ *Then shall a second Lesson be read, taken out of the New Testament.*

¶ *Or else, the first Lesson shall be taken out of an Epistle, or the book of Acts, or the Revelation of St. John, and the second out of a Gospel.*

¶ *Or else, one Lesson only shall be read, taken out of the New Testament.*

THE PRAYERS

¶ *Then shall follow Prayers of Thanksgiving and Intercession, with Commemoration of the Dead (pages 23 to 34). And, if it hath not been done already, Minister and People shall say together the Lord's Prayer.*

¶ *Then shall the Offerings of the People be collected and presented; and, if it be desired, a suitable Anthem may be sung. Or else, the Offerings may be received after the Sermon.*

THE SERMON

¶ *Then shall a Hymn be sung: before or after which such Announcements as are needful and fitting shall be made.*

¶ *Then shall follow the Sermon.*

¶ *Then shall follow thanksgiving for the Word of God, prayer for perseverance in the divine grace, with remembrance of the whole Church of Christ.*

¶ *Then shall a Psalm or Hymn be sung.*

¶ *And the Minister shall let the People depart with the Blessing.*

ANOTHER ORDER FOR

THE PUBLIC WORSHIP OF GOD

ACCORDING TO THE FOREGOING DIRECTORY

THE INTRODUCTION

¶ *The Service shall begin with a Psalm or Hymn of approach to the God of all grace.*

¶ *Then shall the Minister say,*

Let us pray.

O LORD our God, great, eternal, wonderful in glory, who keepest covenant and promise for those that love thee with their whole heart, who art the life of all, the help of those that flee to thee, the hope of those that cry unto thee; Cleanse us from our sins, and from every thought displeasing to thy goodness. Cleanse our souls and bodies, our hearts and consciences, that with pure heart and a clear mind, with perfect love and calm hope, we may confidently and fearlessly pray to thee; through Jesus Christ our Lord. *Amen.*

¶ *Then shall follow this Confession and Prayer for Pardon; the People saying the words of the Confession with the Minister* (*The Hymnary, after No.* 770).

MOST holy and merciful Father; We acknowledge and confess in thy presence, Our sinful nature prone to evil and slothful in good, And all our shortcomings and offences against thee. Thou alone knowest how often we have sinned, In wandering from thy ways, In wasting thy gifts, In forgetting thy love. But thou, O Lord, have pity upon us, Who are ashamed and sorry For all wherein we have displeased thee. Teach us to hate our errors; Cleanse us from our secret faults; And forgive our sins; For the sake of thy dear Son our Saviour. And O most holy and loving Father; Send thy purifying grace into our hearts, we beseech thee; That we may henceforth live in thy light and walk in thy ways; According to the commandments of Jesus Christ our Lord. Amen.

ALMIGHTY God, who dost freely pardon all who repent and turn to thee: Now fulfil in every contrite heart the promise of redeeming grace; remitting all our sins, and cleansing us from an evil conscience; through the perfect sacrifice of Christ our Lord; and keep us evermore in the peace and joy of a holy life; that we may love and serve thee always; through Jesus Christ our Lord. *Amen.*

¶ *Here shall follow a Prayer for Grace contained in this book.*

¶ *Instead of the Confession, Prayer for Pardon, and Prayer for Grace, this Prayer following may be said.*

ALMIGHTY and merciful God, the fountain of all goodness, who knowest the thoughts of our hearts: We confess that we have sinned against thee and done evil in thy sight. Forgive us, O Lord, we beseech thee, and cleanse us from the stains of our former offences. Give us grace and power to put away all hurtful things; so that being delivered from the bondage of sin, we may bring forth fruits worthy of repentance. O eternal Light, shine into our hearts. O eternal Goodness, deliver us from evil. O eternal Power, be our support. O eternal Wisdom, scatter the darkness of our ignorance. Grant unto us, that with all our heart, and mind, and strength, we may evermore seek thy face; and finally bring us in thine infinite mercy to thy holy presence; through Jesus Christ our Lord. *Amen.*

¶ *After which, where it is customary, the Lord's Prayer may be said by Minister and People together.*

OUR Father, who art in heaven, Hallowed be thy name; Thy kingdom come; Thy will be done; In earth as it is in heaven. Give us this day our daily bread. And forgive us our trespasses, As we forgive them that trespass against us. And lead us not into temptation; But deliver us from evil: For thine is the kingdom, The power, and the glory, For ever and ever. Amen.

THE PSALMS

¶ *Then shall one or more Psalms be sung or said, with this Conclusion,*

Glory be to the Father, and to the Son: and to the Holy Ghost; As it was in the beginning, is now, and ever shall be: world without end. Amen.

THE LESSONS

¶ *Then shall a Lesson be read, taken out of the Old Testament.*

¶ *After which a Canticle or a Psalm or a Hymn may be sung.*

¶ *Then shall a second Lesson be read, taken out of the New Testament.*

¶ *Or else, the first Lesson shall be taken out of an Epistle, or the book of Acts, or the Revelation of St. John, and the second out of a Gospel.*

¶ *Or else, one Lesson only shall be read, taken out of the New Testament.*

THE PRAYERS

¶ *Then shall follow Prayers of Thanksgiving and Intercession, with Commemoration of the Dead* (*pages* 23 *to* 34). *And, if it hath not been done already, Minister and People shall say together the Lord's Prayer.*

¶ *Then shall the Offerings of the People be collected and presented; and, if it be desired, a suitable Anthem may be sung. Or else, the Offerings may be received after the Sermon.*

THE SERMON

¶ *Then shall a Hymn be sung; before or after which such Announcements as are needful and fitting shall be made.*

¶ *Then shall follow the Sermon.*

¶ *Then shall follow thanksgiving for the Word of God, prayer for perseverance in the divine grace, with remembrance of the whole Church of Christ.*

¶ *Then shall a Psalm or Hymn be sung.*

¶ *And the Minister shall let the People depart with the Blessing.*

THE SECOND DIRECTORY FOR

THE PUBLIC WORSHIP OF GOD

THE INTRODUCTION

¶ *The Service shall begin with a Psalm or Hymn setting forth the power, the goodness, and the grace of God.*

¶ *Then shall follow Prayer, Minister and People together humbling themselves before God, giving thanks for redemption in Christ, and seeking participation in the fellowship of the redeemed.*

THE WORD OF GOD

¶ *Then shall follow a Prayer for Grace.*

¶ *Then shall be read a Lesson from the Old Testament, or a Lesson from a book of the New Testament other than a Gospel, or from both; he that readeth first saying,* The Lesson is written in the . . . chapter of . . ., beginning at the . . . verse.

¶ *Here a Psalm may be said or sung.*

¶ *Then shall a part of one of the Gospels be read; he that readeth first saying,* The Gospel is written in the . . . chapter of . . ., beginning at the . . . verse. *And after the Gospel shall be said,* Thanks be to thee, O Lord, for this thy glorious Gospel.

¶ *Then shall a Hymn be sung: before or after which such Announcements as are needful and fitting shall be made.*

¶ *Then shall follow the Sermon; the Minister taking his text from the Word of God, and remembering that it is his office to instruct the People in divine truth, to set forth Christ crucified as their Saviour, and to incite them to Christian faith and duty.*

THE FELLOWSHIP OF PRAYER

¶ *The Sermon being ended, the Offerings of the People shall be collected and presented; and a Psalm or a Hymn or a suitable Anthem may be sung.*

¶ *Then shall follow Prayer, the Minister in the name of all, giving praise and thanks to God for all his benefits, and above all for his inestimable love in the redemption of the world by our Saviour Jesus Christ; entreating God of his grace to receive the offering which we now make of ourselves, in union with him who loved us and gave himself for us; making intercession with the Father of mercies for the Church, for the Nation, and the whole family of Mankind, and for all sorts and conditions of men; and remembering with thanksgiving the whole company of the faithful dead who are now at one with him, especially those dear to our own hearts. And then Minister and People shall say together the Lord's Prayer.*

¶ *Then shall a Psalm or a Hymn be sung.*

¶ *And the Minister shall let the People depart with the Blessing.*

AN ORDER FOR
THE PUBLIC WORSHIP OF GOD
ACCORDING TO THE FOREGOING DIRECTORY

THE INTRODUCTION

¶ *The Service shall begin with a Psalm or Hymn shewing forth the power, the goodness, and the grace of God.*

¶ *Then shall the Minister pray in this wise, he and the People humbly seeking the mercy of God.*

ALMIGHTY God, unto whom all hearts be open, all desires known, and from whom no secrets are hid: Cleanse the thoughts of our hearts by the inspiration of thy Holy Spirit, that we may perfectly love thee, and worthily magnify thy holy name; through Christ our Lord. *Amen.*

¶ *Here may follow Confession, or else the Minister shall say,*

O LORD God, hear us when we make our common supplications unto thee.

For the peace that is from above, and for the loving kindness of our God, we make our common supplication unto thee.

For the peace of the whole world, for the well-being of the churches of God and for the unity of them all, we make our common supplication unto thee.

For this house of prayer, and for all that with faith, reverence, and the fear of God enter here, we make our common supplication unto thee.

Remembering what thy love hath wrought in thy saints, and thy faithfulness to our fathers and brethren who are now with thee, we commend ourselves, and one another, and all our life, to Christ our Lord.

Help, save, pity, and defend us, O God, by thy grace. *Amen.*

¶ *Then shall be sung or said this Litany (The Hymnary, No.* 758).

Lord, have mercy.
Christ, have mercy.
Lord, have mercy.

¶ *Then shall be sung or said* Gloria in excelsis (*The Hymnary, No.* 750), *or* Benedictus (*The Hymnary,* No. 753); *or else a Hymn of praise and humble gratitude to God.*

THE WORD OF GOD

¶ *Then shall follow a Prayer for Grace.*

¶ *Then shall be read a Lesson from the Old Testament, or a Lesson from a book of the New Testament other than a Gospel, or from both.*

¶ *Here a Psalm or part of a Psalm may be said or sung.*

¶ *Then shall a part of one of the Gospels be read.*

¶ *Then shall a Hymn be sung; before or after which such Announcements as are needful and fitting shall be made.*

¶ *Then shall follow the Sermon.*

THE FELLOWSHIP OF PRAYER

¶ *The Sermon being ended, the Offerings of the People shall be collected and presented; and a Psalm or a Hymn or a suitable Anthem may be sung.*

¶ *Then shall follow Prayers of Thanksgiving and Intercession, with Commemoration of the Dead* (*pages* 23 *to* 34). *And Minister and People shall say together the Lord's Prayer.*

¶ *Then shall a Psalm or a Hymn be sung.*

¶ *And the Minister shall let the People depart with the Blessing.*

ANOTHER ORDER FOR

THE PUBLIC WORSHIP OF GOD

ACCORDING TO THE FOREGOING DIRECTORY

THE INTRODUCTION

¶ *The Service shall begin with a Psalm or Hymn setting forth the power, the goodness, and the grace of God.*

¶ *Then shall follow this Prayer,*

O LORD our God, who hast brought us once more to thy house of prayer, to praise thy goodness and ask for thy grace: Accept now in thy endless mercy, the sacrifice of our worship and thanksgiving, and grant unto us all such requests as may be wholesome for us. Make us to be children of the light and of the day, and heirs of thy everlasting inheritance. Remember, O Lord, according to the multitude of thy mercies, thy whole Church, all who join with us in prayer, all our brethren by land and sea, or wherever they may be in thy vast kingdom, who stand in need of thy grace and succour. Pour out upon them the riches of thy mercy, so that we, redeemed in soul and body, and steadfast in faith, may ever praise thy wonderful and holy name; through Jesus Christ our Lord. *Amen.*

¶ *Then shall follow a Hymn of praise and humble gratitude to God.*

THE PUBLIC WORSHIP OF GOD

THE WORD OF GOD

¶ *Then shall follow a Prayer for Grace.*

¶ *Then shall be read a Lesson from the Old Testament, or a Lesson from a book of the New Testament other than a Gospel, or from both.*

¶ *Here a Psalm or part of a Psalm may be said or sung.*

¶ *Then shall a part of one of the Gospels be read.*

¶ *Then shall a Hymn be sung; before or after which such Announcements as are needful and fitting shall be made.*

¶ *Then shall follow the Sermon.*

THE FELLOWSHIP OF PRAYER

¶ *The Sermon being ended, the Offerings of the People shall be collected and presented; and a Psalm or a Hymn or a suitable Anthem may be sung.*

¶ *Then shall follow Prayers of Thanksgiving and Intercession, with Commemoration of the Dead (pages 23 to 34). And Minister and People shall say together the Lord's Prayer.*

¶ *Then shall a Psalm or a Hymn be sung.*

¶ *And the Minister shall let the People depart with the Blessing.*

A DIRECTORY FOR
AN EVENING SERVICE

THE INTRODUCTION

¶ *The Service shall begin with a Psalm or Hymn of approach to the God of all grace; and then the Minister shall lead the people in Prayers of Invocation, of Confession, and of Supplication; after which, where it is customary, Minister and People may say together the Lord's Prayer.*

THE PSALMS

¶ *Then may one or more Psalms be sung or said, with this Conclusion,*

Glory be to the Father, and to the Son: and to the Holy Ghost; As it was in the beginning, is now, and ever shall be: world without end. Amen.

THE LESSONS

¶ *Then shall a Lesson be read, taken out of the Holy Scripture.*

¶ *Before the Lesson is read the Minister shall say,* Let us hear the Word of God, as it is contained in such a book, such a chapter, beginning at such a verse; *and after the Lesson,* The Lord bless to us the reading of his Holy Word, and to his name be glory and praise.

¶ *Or else, he shall say before the Lesson,* Here beginneth such a chapter, *or* such a verse of such a chapter, of such a book; *and after the Lesson,* Here endeth the Lesson.

¶ *After which a Canticle or a suitable Psalm or Hymn may be sung.*

THE PRAYERS

¶ *Then shall follow this or some other similar Prayer of Thanksgiving and Intercession.*

ALMIGHTY God, our heavenly Father, we give thee praise and thanks that unto us the unworthy thou hast drawn near in thy Son, Jesus Christ. We praise thee for his loving kindness and tender mercy. We thank thee that in him we know thee as our Father and one another as thy children. Thou hast redeemed our lives from destruction. Thou hast opened thy hand and satisfied us with good things. Grant that what thou hast sown in love may spring up in service, and that by thy grace we may walk in the paths of righteousness.

Blessed Lord, who hast given us a new commandment that we should love one another even as thou didst love us: Give unto us thy servants grace, that we may be kindly affectioned one to another. And hasten, we humbly beseech thee, the day when with one heart and mind all men shall come to a knowledge of thy love.

Have mercy, O Lord, upon thy whole Church, that it may be faithful to its trust and fearless in proclaiming the Gospel. Heal the divisions which hinder its witness and unite all thy people in the bonds of a common faith and love.

Have mercy, O Lord, upon all thy children, especially those who take counsel together, that justice, mercy, and peace may prevail and thy name be glorified. Grant thy heavenly wisdom to our King and all who are set in authority under him. Let righteousness be the strength of our nation and commonwealth that we may walk worthy of the high calling to which thou hast called us.

Have mercy, O Lord, upon all who have special need of thee this night. Sustain those who are in trouble; strengthen those who are tempted; uphold those who falter; heal those who are sick; go with those who enter the valley of the shadow, and comfort those who mourn; that all may know thy power and be enabled by thy grace to endure.

O Lord, support us all the day long of this troublous life, until the shadows lengthen, and the evening comes, and the busy world is hushed, and the fever of life is over, and our work is done. Then of thy tender mercy grant us a safe lodging, and a holy rest, and peace at the last; through Jesus Christ our Lord. *Amen.*

¶ *And then, if it hath not been said already, Minister and People shall say together the Lord's Prayer.*

¶ *Then shall the Offerings of the People be collected and presented; and, if it be desired, a suitable Anthem may be sung. Or else, the Offerings may be received after the Sermon.*

THE SERMON

¶ *Then shall a Hymn be sung; before or after which such Announcements as are needful and fitting shall be made.*

¶ *Then shall follow the Sermon, the Minister taking his text from the Word of God, and remembering that it is his office to instruct the People in divine truth, to set forth Christ crucified as their Saviour, and to incite them to Christian faith and duty.*

¶ *Then shall follow thanksgiving for the Word of God, prayer for perseverance in the divine grace, with remembrance of the whole Church of Christ.*

¶ *Then shall a Psalm or Hymn be sung.*

¶ *And the Minister shall let the People depart with the Blessing.*

PRAYERS AND THANKSGIVINGS FOR PUBLIC WORSHIP

Which may be used with either Directory, or with any Order based thereon.

One Prayer may be taken from each group following.

1. *Invocation.*

ALMIGHTY God, from whom every good prayer cometh: Deliver us, when we draw nigh to thee, from coldness of heart and wanderings of mind, that with steadfast thought and kindled desire we may worship thee in the faith and spirit of Jesus Christ our Lord. *Amen.*

ALMIGHTY God, our heavenly Father, in whom alone our hearts find rest and peace: We beseech thee to reveal thyself to us in this hour of worship; pour down upon us thy spiritual gifts; and grant that this season of holy quiet may be profitable to us in heavenly things, and refresh and strengthen us to finish the work which thou hast given us to do; through Jesus Christ our Lord. *Amen.*

2. *Adoration.*

ETERNAL and ever-blessed God, we bow before thy Divine Majesty, adoring thee, the Lord of heaven and earth, of whom and through whom and to whom are all things; unto whom be glory for ever and ever. *Amen.*

O THOU who art beyond our sight, above our thought, infinite, eternal, and unsearchable: Thy wisdom shines in all thy works; thy glory is shown in thy goodness to men; and thy grace and truth are revealed in Christ. Therefore we adore thee, our Father and our God, for ever and ever. *Amen.*

ALMIGHTY God, most blessed and most holy, before the brightness of whose presence the angels veil their faces: With lowly reverence and adoring love we acknowledge thine infinite glory, and worship Thee, Father, Son, and Holy Spirit, eternal Trinity. Blessing, and honour, and glory, and power be unto our God, for ever and ever. *Amen.*

TO God the Father, who first loved us and made us acceptable in the Beloved; to God the Son, who loved us and gave himself for us; to God the Holy Spirit, who sheds the love of God abroad in our hearts: be all love and glory for time and eternity. *Amen.*

GLORY be to God in the highest, the creator and Lord of heaven and earth, the preserver of all things, the Father of mercies, who so loved mankind as to send his only begotten Son into the world, to redeem us from sin and misery, and to obtain for us everlasting life. Accept, O gracious God, our praises and our thanksgiving for thine infinite mercies toward us. And teach us, O Lord, to love thee more and serve thee better; through Jesus Christ our Lord. *Amen.*

3. *Thanksgiving.*

ALMIGHTY God, Father of all mercies, We thine unworthy servants do give thee most humble and hearty thanks For all thy goodness and loving kindness to us, and to all men. We bless thee for our creation, preservation, and all the blessings of this life; But above all for thine inestimable love In the redemption of the world by our Lord Jesus Christ; For the means of grace, And for the hope of glory. And, we beseech thee, give us that due sense of all thy mercies, That our hearts may be unfeignedly thankful, And that we show forth thy praise, Not only with our lips, but in our lives; By giving up ourselves to thy service, And by walking before thee in holiness and righteousness all our days; Through Jesus Christ our Lord, To whom with thee and the Holy Spirit be all honour and glory, world without end. *Amen.* (*This Prayer may be said by Minister and People together, as in The Hymnary after* 770).

MOST heartily do we thank thee, O Lord, for all thy mercies of every kind, and for thy loving care over all thy creatures. We bless thee for the gift of life, for thy protection round about us, for thy guiding hand upon us, and for the many tokens of thy love; especially for the saving knowledge of thy dear Son, our Redeemer; and for the living presence of thy Spirit, our Comforter. We thank thee for friendship and duty, for good hopes and precious memories, for the joys that cheer us, and for the trials that teach us to trust in thee. Take from us everything that would hide the light of thy countenance; and enable us to give ourselves entirely to thy will, who art our Creator and Lord; through Jesus Christ our Lord. *Amen.*

MOST gracious God, who hast opened thy hand to give us all good things: Thou keepest us beneath the shadow of thy wings; thou providest for us as a father; thou lovest us as a friend, and thinkest on us every day. Unto thee, O Lord, we offer praise for our redemption in Christ. Grant now that what thou hast sown in loving kindness may spring up in service; let thy grace strengthen our purpose to do always what is pleasing in thy sight; living here in the light of thy favour, may we at last enter into thy glory, and give thanks to thee for ever. *Amen.*

ALMIGHTY God, our most gracious Father in heaven, who hast ever watched over us in thy providence and love, and who hast blessed us with all spiritual blessings in Christ Jesus; we thank thee for thine untold mercies.

We bless thee for the order and beauty of all that thou hast made: for the wonder of the world about us; for day and night, for summer and winter, for sun and rain, for seed-time and harvest, and for thy bountiful supply of all our needs.

We bless thee for thy goodness to us

throughout the days of our earthly life; for protecting us in our weakness; for increasing and renewing our strength; for fitting us for the conflict with evil and sin; and for calling us into thy service and into the knowledge of thy truth.

We bless thee for all whom thou hast given to be near and dear to us: for those united to us in the sacred ties of family life; for our friends and comrades; for our pastors and teachers; and for all with whom we are joined in the covenant of thy Church.

We bless thee, most of all, for sending thy Son to be our Saviour: for his taking of our nature; for his life on earth; for his sufferings and death upon the Cross; for his resurrection and reign; and for his gift of the Holy Spirit. Thanks be to thee, that he bore our sins in his own body on the tree, and opened for us the gateway of life eternal.

Grant, O God, that our hearts may grow in thankfulness for thy mercies; and enable us, by thy grace, to give all that we have and are for thy service, to the glory of thy name; through Jesus Christ our Lord. *Amen.*

THANKS be to thee, O Lord Jesus Christ, for all the benefits which thou hast given us; for all the pains and insults which thou hast borne for us. O most merciful Redeemer, Friend and Brother, may we know thee more clearly, love thee more dearly, and follow thee more nearly; for thine own sake. *Amen.*

O LORD our heavenly Father, we thank thee for all thy mercies to us and to all men; but above all we bless thee for that thou hast made us in thine own image, redeemed us from death by the life of thy blessed Son, and consecrated us by thy holy and life-giving Spirit; and, we beseech thee, grant us grace so to live before thee here with true and honest hearts that at length we may have our place in the everlasting country, where, with the Son and the Holy Spirit, thou ever livest and reignest, one God, for ever and ever. *Amen.*

4. *Intercession.*

O GOD, the Creator and Preserver of all mankind, we humbly beseech thee for all sorts and conditions of men; that thou wouldst be pleased to make thy ways known unto them, thy saving health unto all nations. More especially, we pray for the good estate of the Catholic Church; that it may be so guided and governed by thy good Spirit, that all who profess and call themselves Christians may be led into the way of truth, and hold the faith in unity of spirit, in the bond of peace, and in righteousness of life. Finally, we commend to thy fatherly goodness all those, who are any ways afflicted, or distressed, in mind, body, or estate; especially those for whom our prayers are asked at this time; that it may please thee to comfort and relieve them, according to their several necessities, giving them patience under their sufferings, and a happy issue out of all their afflictions. And this we beg for Jesus Christ's sake. *Amen.*

O GOD, who art mindful of thy children everywhere: Reveal thy mercy unto all men, and remember in thy great good will, those for whom we now make intercession. Remember thy Church which thou hast purchased of old; and let all the ends of the earth see the salvation of our God. Remember our nation which thou hast established; give wisdom and power to thy servants on whom thou hast laid the burden of authority, especially the King and his counsellors and all judges; and unite the whole body of the commonwealth to promote the peace and welfare of the world. Remember all the persecuted and afflicted; strengthen the weak, confirm the strong, instruct the ignorant, deliver the oppressed, heal the sick, relieve the needy that hath no helper; and lead us all by the waters of comfort, and in the ways of righteousness, to thine everlasting rest; through Jesus Christ our Lord. *Amen.*

O GOD, who art the hope of all the ends of the earth: Remember the whole creation, pity our race, and save the world from sin. Protect our land from whatever threatens her welfare, so that religion and virtue may flourish more and more. Give the spirit of wisdom and godly fear to thy servant King George, and all who are in authority over us.

Give humility to the rich, and grace to use their riches to thy glory; bless the people in their callings and families, and be thou a refuge to the poor in their distress. Make every home a shelter from temptation and a nursery of noble youth; take also the homeless beneath thy protection. Cleanse and sanctify the Church which thou hast loved; and reveal the Spirit of thy Son through the life and service of thy people. Enlighten all who are perplexed in faith, support those who are tempted, awaken those who sleep, comfort the afflicted, and encourage such as are ready to faint. Encompass with thy favour all whose lives thou hast bound up with our own; and, if there be any who do us wrong, remove all bitterness from our hearts while we pray for thy blessing upon them. Give peace, O Lord, in our time, and unite all hearts in the love of thy dear Son, Jesus Christ our Lord. *Amen.*

ALMIGHTY God, who hast taught us to make intercession for all men: We pray not only for ourselves here present, but we beseech thee also to bring all such as know thee not from the captivity of error to the understanding of thy heavenly truth; that we all, with one consent and unity of mind, may worship thee, our only God and Saviour; that all thy ministers and people may both in their life and doctrine be found faithful: and that, by them, all poor sheep which wander and go astray, may be gathered and brought home to thy fold.

Moreover, because the reins of government are in thy hands, we beseech thee to direct and bless all who are in lawful authority; especially thy servant King George, and all others to whom thou hast entrusted power, together with the whole body of the people. Let thy fatherly favour so preserve them, and thy Holy Spirit so govern their hearts, that religion may be purely maintained, and our land may abide in righteousness and peace.

Finally we beseech thee for all those who are called to bear any cross or tribulation; that it may please thee to sustain them with the comfort of thy Holy Spirit, until thou send a full deliverance out of all their troubles; so that through their patience and constancy thy kingdom may increase and shine through all the world. And these, with all other mercies, we humbly beg of thee, in the name of Jesus Christ, thy Son, our Lord. *Amen.*

A Litany

Minister. For the peace that is from above and for the loving kindness of our God,

People. Lord have mercy and hear our prayer.

Minister. For the peace of the whole world, for the well-being of the Churches of God and for the unity of them all,

People. Lord have mercy and hear our prayer.

Minister. For this house of prayer, and for all that with faith, reverence, and the fear of God enter here,

People. Lord have mercy and hear our prayer.

Minister. For the Moderator of the United Church of Canada, for all who serve in the work of the ministry, and for all faithful people,

People. Lord have mercy and hear our prayer.

Minister. For the Dominion of Canada and the British Commonwealth of nations, for our sovereign Lord the King and all who are set in authority under him,

People. Lord have mercy and hear our prayer.

Minister. For the place in which we live, for every city and land, and for all the faithful who dwell therein,

People. Lord have mercy and hear our prayer.

Minister. For seasonable weather, for an abundance of the fruits of the earth and for peaceful times.

People. Lord have mercy and hear our prayer.

Minister. For those who travel by land or sea or air, for the sick and the suffering, or the exiled and those who are persecuted for righteousness' sake,

People. Lord have mercy and hear our prayer.

Minister. Remembering what thy love hath wrought in thy saints. and thy faithfulness to our fathers and brethren who are now with thee; we commend ourselves and one another, and all our life, to Christ our Lord.

People. Help, save, pity, and defend us, O God, by thy grace. Amen.

¶ *Other Prayers of Intercession may be found on pages* 124 *to* 127.

5. *Commemoration of the Blessed Dead.*

O GOD, before whose face the generations rise and pass away; the strength of those who labour and suffer, and the repose of the holy and blessed dead: We rejoice in the communion of thy saints. We remember all who have faithfully lived; all who have peacefully died, and especially those most dear to us. Lift us into light and love; and give us at last our portion with those who have trusted in thee, and striven in all things to do thy holy will. And unto thy name, with the Church on earth and the Church in heaven, would we ascribe all honour and glory, world without end. *Amen.*

O LORD, the God of mercy, unto whom all live, and who dost vouchsafe unto the souls of the faithful departed, a place of refreshment, blessed rest, and perfect release from all sin and sorrow where the light of thy presence shineth for evermore: Grant, we beseech thee, that we may be united with them in the bliss of thine eternal glory; through Jesus Christ our Lord. *Amen.*

O GOD of the spirits of all flesh, we praise and magnify thy holy name for all thy servants who have finished their course in thy faith and fear, whether known to us or unknown; and we beseech thee that, encouraged by their examples, and strengthened by their fellowship, we also may be found meet to be partakers of the inheritance of the saints in light; through the merits of thy Son Jesus Christ our Lord. *Amen.*

O ETERNAL Lord God, who holdest all souls in life: We beseech thee to shed forth upon thy whole Church the bright beams of thy light and heavenly comfort; and grant that we, following the good example of those who have loved and served thee here and are now at rest, may at the last enter with them into the fullness of thine unending joy; through Jesus Christ our Lord. *Amen.*

ALMIGHTY and Eternal God, who for thine own glory and their exceeding peace, hast guided the feet of thy saints through the devious pathways of this world, and brought them to a better country: We, who yet walk in the paths of this earthly life, humbly beseech thee that thou wilt so guide us by thy Holy Spirit, that in thy mercy we may come at last to that place of peace, where dwell all those whom thy love hath redeemed; through Jesus Christ our Lord. *Amen.*

¶ *Other Prayers of Commemoration of the Blessed Dead may be found on page* 200.

FOR THE CHURCH

MOST gracious Father, we humbly beseech thee for thy holy Catholic Church. Fill it with all truth; in all truth with all peace. Where it is corrupt, purge it; where it is in error, direct it; where anything is amiss, reform it; where it is right, strengthen and confirm it; where it is in want, furnish it; where it is divided and rent asunder, make up the breaches of it, O thou Holy One of Israel. *Amen.*

O GOD of unchangeable power and eternal light, look favourably upon thy whole Church, that wonderful and sacred mystery; and by the tranquil operation of thy perpetual providence carry out the work of man's salvation; that things which were cast down may be raised up, and that all things may come to perfection through him by whom all things were made, even thy Son Jesus Christ our Lord. *Amen.*

O LORD, the splendour of eternal light and the sun of justice: Give thy blessing on all states and conditions in thy holy Church. To them that teach grant the gifts of knowledge, discernment, and love; to them that minister in holy things to be humble, tender, and pure; to all pastors of thy flock to be zealous, vigilant, and unworldly, having their hearts set upon invisible things. Grant to our heads of families to be wise and gentle, to our young people to be prudent and chaste, to our old people to be cheerful and fervent, to all who are engaged in business to be honest and unselfish. Build us up in faith, hope, charity, and all virtues; through Jesus Christ our Lord. *Amen.*

O ALMIGHTY God, who hast built thy Church upon the foundation of the Apostles and Prophets, Jesus Christ himself being the head corner stone: Grant us so to be joined together in unity of spirit by their doctrine, that we may be made an holy temple acceptable unto thee; through Jesus Christ our Lord. *Amen.*

FOR THE UNITY OF ALL CHRISTIAN PEOPLE

O LORD Jesus Christ, who didst say to thine Apostles, Peace I leave with you, my peace I give unto you: Regard not our sins, but the faith of thy Church, and grant her that peace and unity which is agreeable to thy will; who livest and reignest with the Father and the Holy Spirit, one God, world without end. *Amen.*

O LORD, the Father of our Lord Jesus Christ, our only Saviour, the Prince of Peace: Give us grace seriously to lay to heart the great dangers we are in by our unhappy divisions. Take away all hatred and prejudice, and whatsoever else may hinder us from godly union and concord: that, as there is but one Body, and one Spirit, and one hope of our calling, one Lord, one faith, one baptism, one God and Father of us all, so we may henceforth be all of one heart, and of one soul, united in one holy bond of truth and peace, of faith and charity, and may with one mind and one mouth glorify thee; through Jesus Christ our Lord. *Amen.*

FOR MINISTERS

REMEMBER all them that do the Lord's work in the ministry and conduct of souls. Give them, we beseech thee, O Father, great gifts and great holiness, that wisely and charitably, diligently and zealously, prudently and acceptably, they may be guides to the blind, and comforters to the sad and weary; that they may strengthen the weak and confirm the strong, separate the worthless from the precious, boldly rebuke sin, patiently suffer for the truth, and be exemplary in their lives; that in all their actions and sermons, in their discipline and ministrations, they may advance the good of souls, and the honour of our Lord Jesus Christ; Grant this for the sake of thy Son our Lord. *Amen.*

FOR MINISTERS AND PEOPLE

O ALMIGHTY God, who by thy Son Jesus Christ didst give to thy Apostle Saint Peter many excellent gifts, and commandedst him earnestly to feed thy flock: Make, we beseech thee, all Ministers of thy Church diligently to preach thy holy Word, and the people obediently to follow the same, that they may receive the crown of everlasting glory; through Jesus Christ our Lord. *Amen.*

ALMIGHTY and everlasting God, who alone workest great marvels: Send down upon thy Ministers and all Congregations committed to their charge, the healthful spirit of thy grace; and that they may truly please thee pour upon them the continual dew of thy blessing. Grant this, O Lord, for the honour of our Advocate and Mediator, Jesus Christ. *Amen.*

FOR THE PASTORAL CHARGE

ALMIGHTY and everlasting God, who dost govern all things in heaven and earth: Mercifully hear the supplications of us thy servants; and grant unto the people of this place all things needful for their spiritual welfare. Strengthen and confirm the faithful; protect and guide the children; visit and relieve the sick and afflicted; turn and soften the wicked; rouse the careless; recover the fallen; restore the penitent; remove all hindrances to the advancement of thy truth; and bring all to be of one heart and mind within the fold of thy holy Church; to the honour and glory of thy blessed name; through Jesus Christ our Lord. *Amen.*

FOR CHURCH WORK

O LORD, without whom our labour is but lost, and with whom thy little ones go forth as the mighty: Be present at all works in thy Church which are undertaken according to thy will (*especially* . . .), and grant to thy labourers a pure intention, patient faith, sufficient success upon earth, and the bliss of serving thee in heaven; through Jesus Christ our Lord. *Amen.*

O GOD, who hast given unto thy servants diversities of gifts by the same Spirit, and hast taught us by thy holy Apostle that all our doings without charity are nothing worth: Be pleased to bless and prosper all who love and serve their fellow-men with a pure heart fervently, remembering the poor, healing the sick, comforting the sorrowful, teaching the ignorant, and lifting up the afflicted; let their prayers and alms come up for a memorial before thee; and reward them plentifully with peace; through the merits of Jesus Christ our only Saviour. *Amen.*

FOR HOME AND KINDRED

O GOD, our heavenly Father, who hast set the solitary in families: Look in favour, we beseech thee, upon the homes of thy people. Defend them against all evil, and supply all their needs according to the riches of thy grace. Make them sanctuaries of purity and peace, love and joy. O thou protector and friend, keep all our dear ones within the safe shelter of thy love. May they and we follow thee at every step of our daily life, and though our paths may lead us far from one another may we all be led at last to thee; through Jesus Christ our Lord. *Amen.*

FOR THE CHILDREN

O HEAVENLY Father, who long ago didst watch thy Son on earth grow as in stature so in wisdom and in perfect love of thee: Teach by the wondrous tale of Jesus and his Church the children whom thou watchest now; that they may grow into his likeness, loving thee, obedient to thy will, and happy in thy house; through the same Jesus Christ our Lord. *Amen.*

FOR SCHOOLS AND COLLEGES

O GOD, the eternal wisdom, who wouldest all should learn to know and see thee in the splendour of thy Son's life on earth: Grant that our universities and schools, first learning Christ, may impart full treasures of knowledge, truth and faith; so that both Church and Commonwealth be nobly served by lives which follow his; who liveth and reigneth with thee and the Holy Spirit, one God, world without end. *Amen.*

ALMIGHTY God, of whose gift cometh wisdom and understanding: We beseech thee with thy gracious favour to behold our universities, colleges, and schools, that the confines of knowledge may be ever enlarged, and all good learning flourish and abound. Bless all who teach and all who learn; and grant that both teachers and learners in humility of heart may look ever upwards unto thee, who art the fountain of all wisdom; through Jesus our Lord, who liveth and reigneth with thee in the unity of the Holy Spirit, world without end. *Amen.*

FOR THE RIGHT USE OF SUNDAY

LORD, who dost ask of thy people love for love, and worship in return for life: Assist us to keep holy, week by week, the day of thy Son's mighty rising from the dead, and bless us in the breaking of the bread and the prayers; that other thy children who behold our joy may seek thy loving kindness in the midst of thy temple; through the same Jesus Christ our Lord. *Amen.*

O GOD, who makest us glad with the weekly remembrance of the glorious resurrection of thy Son our Lord: Vouchsafe us this day such a blessing through thy worship, that the days which follow it may be spent in thy favour; through the same Jesus Christ our Lord. *Amen.*

FOR THE WORD OF GOD

BLESSED Lord, by whose providence all Holy Scriptures were written and preserved for our instruction: Give us grace to study them this and every day, with patience and love. Strengthen our souls with the fullness of their divine teaching. Keep from us all pride and irreverence. Guide us in the deep things of thy heavenly wisdom, and of thy great mercy lead us by thy Word unto everlasting life; through Jesus Christ our Lord and Saviour. *Amen.*

O GOD, whose Word is quick and powerful, and sharper than any two-edged sword: Grant unto us who are here before thee that we may receive thy truth into our hearts, in faith and love. By it may we be taught and guided, upheld and comforted; that we be no longer children in understanding, but grow to the stature of perfect men in Christ, and be prepared unto every good word and work, to the honour of thy name; through Jesus Christ our Lord. *Amen.*

FOR THE MISSIONARY WORK OF THE CHURCH

O GOD of all the nations of the earth, remember the multitudes of the heathen, who, though created in thine image, have not known thee, nor the dying of thy Son their Saviour Jesus Christ; and grant that by the prayers and labours of thy holy Church they may be delivered from all superstition and unbelief and brought to worship thee; through him whom thou hast sent to be the resurrection and the life of all men, the same thy Son Jesus Christ our Lord. *Amen.*

O GOD, who hast made of one blood all nations of men for to dwell on the face of the earth, and didst send thy blessed Son Jesus Christ to preach peace to them that are afar off, and to them that are nigh: Grant that all the peoples of the world may feel after thee and find thee; and hasten, O Lord, the fulfilment of thy promise, to pour out thy Spirit upon all flesh; through Jesus Christ our Lord. *Amen.*

ALMIGHTY and everlasting God, who hast wrought the redemption of man after a miraculous manner, in sending thy only Son to fulfil the promises made unto our fathers: Open up more and more the knowledge of that salvation, that in all places of the earth thy truth and power may be made known, to the intent that all nations may praise, honour, and glorify thee; through the self-same Son, Jesus Christ. *Amen.*

ALMIGHTY God, who hast called the Church out of the world that she might bring the world to thee: Make her faithful, we beseech thee, in the work thou hast entrusted to her hands. Bless and uphold thy servants who are gone forth in her name to preach the Gospel in distant lands; be with them in all perils by land or by water, in weariness and painfulness, in discouragement and persecution; endue them with power from on high. Stir up the hearts of thy people here and everywhere, that by their prayers, gifts, and labours, they may have due part in the spreading of thy Gospel over all the earth; and hasten the time when all the ends of the world shall remember and turn unto the Lord, and all the kindreds of the nations shall worship before thee; through Jesus Christ our Lord. *Amen.*

O LORD, who hast warned us that thou wilt require much of those to whom much is given: Grant that we, whose lot is cast in so goodly a heritage, may strive together the more abundantly, by our prayers, labours, and gifts, to extend to those who know thee not what we so richly enjoy; and as we have entered into the labours of others, so to labour that others may enter into ours, to the fulfilment of thy holy will, and the salvation of all mankind; through Jesus Christ our Lord. *Amen.*

FOR CHURCH COURTS

ALMIGHTY God, who through the Apostles of thy Son Jesus Christ didst order the governance of thy flock: Send now thy blessing upon this Court of thy Church, assembled in thy name. Forasmuch as thou hast called us to serve thee, grant that we may be faithful stewards. Help us to hallow thy name by our reverence for the things that thou lovest, and to guard our trust by our love to one another and to thee. Direct and govern us by thy Holy Spirit, preserving us from hasty judgment and vain dispute, guiding us both to devise and do those things which shall be for the good of thy Church and the glory of thy Son, our only King and Saviour. *Amen.*

ALMIGHTY and everlasting God, who hast promised to be with thy Church alway unto the end of the world: Vouchsafe, we pray thee, unto thy servants assembled in this place, thy gracious presence and blessing. Deliver them from all error, pride, and prejudice; enlighten them with wisdom from above; and so order all their doings, that thy kingdom may be advanced, and all thy ministers and congregations established in their most holy faith; until at length all thy people shall be gathered into one fold of the great Shepherd, Jesus Christ our Lord; to whom be glory for ever. *Amen.*

FOR THE KING AND ALL IN AUTHORITY UNDER HIM

O LORD our heavenly Father, high and mighty, King of kings, Lord of lords, the only Ruler of princes, who dost from thy throne behold all the dwellers upon earth: Most heartily we beseech thee with thy favour to behold our most gracious Sovereign Lord, King George; and so replenish him with the grace of thy Holy Spirit, that he may alway incline to thy will, and walk in thy way. Endue him plenteously with heavenly gifts; grant him in health and wealth long to live; strengthen him that he may vanquish and overcome all his enemies; and finally, after this life, he may attain everlasting joy and felicity; through Jesus Christ our Lord. *Amen.*

ALMIGHTY God, the fountain of all goodness, we humbly beseech thee to bless our Sovereign Lord, King George, the Parliaments in all his dominions, and all who are set in authority under him; that they may order all things in wisdom, righteousness, and peace, to the honour of thy holy name, and the good of thy Church and people; through Jesus Christ our Lord. *Amen.*

FOR THE ROYAL FAMILY

ALMIGHTY God, the fountain of all goodness, we humbly beseech thee to bless her Majesty the Queen, the Queen Mother, the Princess *Elizabeth*, and all the Royal Family. Endue them with thy Holy Spirit; enrich them with thy heavenly grace; prosper them with all happiness; and bring them to thine everlasting kingdom; through Jesus Christ our Lord. *Amen.*

FOR THE EMPIRE

ALMIGHTY God, who hast joined in a single Empire divers peoples and far-sundered lands under our Sovereign Lord, King George: Cause thou that liberty, peace and joy inhabit all its bounds; and bind it one in service to mankind and loyalty to thee; through Jesus Christ our Lord. *Amen.*

LORD, bless this Kingdom and Empire, that religion and virtue may flourish among us, that there may be peace within our gates, and prosperity in all our borders. In time of trouble guide us, and in peace may we not forget thee; and whether in plenty or in want, may all things be so ordered, that we may patiently and peaceably seek thy kingdom and its righteousness, the only full supply and sure foundation both of men and states; so that we may continue a place and people to do thee service to the end of time; through Jesus Christ our only Saviour and Redeemer. *Amen.*

ALMIGHTY God, of whose righteous will all things are, and were created: Thou hast gathered our people into a great nation, and sent them to sow beside all waters, and multiply sure dwellings on the earth. Deepen the root of our life in everlasting righteousness. Make us equal to our high trusts, reverent in the use of freedom, just in the exercise of power, generous in the protection of weakness. With all thy blessings, bless thy servant George, our King, with all members of the Royal House. Fill his heart and theirs with such loyalty to thee, that his people may be exalted by their loyalty to him. To our legislators and councillors give insight and faithfulness, that our laws may clearly speak the right, and our judges purely interpret them. May wisdom and knowledge be the stability of our times, and our deepest trust be in thee, the Lord of nations, and the King of kings; through Jesus Christ our Lord. *Amen.*

FOR THE DOMINION OF CANADA

ALMIGHTY God, who didst lead our fathers into this land, and set their feet in a large room: Give thy grace, we beseech thee, to us their children, that we may approve ourselves a people mindful of thy favour, and glad to do thy will. Bless our Dominion with honourable industry, sound learning, and pure manners. Save us from lawlessness and discord, pride and arrogance, and fashion into one godly people the multitude brought hither out of many kindreds and tongues. Give to all the spirit of service, love, and mutual forbearance. In prosperity make us thankful unto thee, and in the day of trouble suffer not our trust in thee to fail. So that, loving thee above all things, we may fulfil thy gracious purpose in this land; through Jesus Christ our Lord. *Amen.*

FOR THE HIGH COURT OF PARLIAMENT

MOST gracious God, we humbly beseech thee for the High Court of Parliament at this time assembled, that thou wouldest be pleased to direct and prosper all their counsels, to the advancement of thy glory, the good of thy Church, and the safety, honour, and welfare of this Dominion; to the end that peace and happiness, truth and justice, religion and piety, may be established among us for all generations; through Jesus Christ our Lord. *Amen.*

AT THE TIME OF AN ELECTION

ALMIGHTY God, the source of all wisdom: Direct, we beseech thee, the minds of those now called to elect fit persons to serve in the High Court of Parliament (*or* the Council of this . . . ; *or as may be required*); that they may have regard to thy glory and the welfare of thy people; and on those whom they shall choose, bestow, of thy goodness, the spirit of wisdom and true religion; for the sake of our Lord and Saviour Jesus Christ. *Amen.*

FOR THE LABOURS OF MEN

PROSPER our industries, we pray thee, God most high, that our land may be full with all manner of store, and there be no complaining in our streets; and, as thy glorious Son our Lord plied tools on earth, so give to all that labour pride in their work, a just reward, and joy both in supplying need and serving thee; through the same Jesus Christ our Lord. *Amen.*

ALMIGHTY God, who hast blessed the earth that it should be fruitful and bring forth abundantly whatsoever is needful for the life of man: Prosper, we beseech thee, the labours of the husbandman, and grant such seasonable weather that we may gather in the fruits of the earth, and ever rejoice in thy goodness, to the praise of thy holy name; through Jesus Christ our Lord. *Amen.*

THANKSGIVING FOR THE HARVEST

O LORD God Almighty, the Creator and Father of all: We yield thee hearty thanks that thou hast ordained for mankind both seed-time and harvest, and dost now bestow upon us thy children the fruits of the earth in their season. For these and all other thy mercies we laud and magnify thy glorious name; through Jesus Christ our Lord. *Amen.*

ALMIGHTY God and heavenly Father, we glorify thee that we are once more permitted to enjoy the fulfilment of thy gracious promise, that, while the earth remaineth, seed-time and harvest shall not fail. Blessed be thou, who hast given us the fruits of the earth in their season. Teach us to remember that it is not by bread alone that man doth live; but grant that we may feed on him who is the true bread which cometh down from heaven, even Jesus Christ, our Lord and Saviour; to whom, with thee, O Father, and thee, O Holy Spirit, be honour and glory, for ever and ever. *Amen.*

FOR SEAFARERS

O ETERNAL Lord God, who alone spreadest out the heavens, and rulest the raging of the sea: Be pleased to receive into thy protection all those who go down to the sea in ships, and occupy their business in great waters. Preserve them both in body and soul; prosper their labours with good success; in all time of danger be their defence, and bring them to the haven where they would be; through Jesus Christ our Lord. *Amen.*

ALMIGHTY God, who hast made the sea and all that moveth therein: Bestow thy blessing on the harvest of the waters, that it may be abundant in its season, and on our fishermen and mariners, that they may be safe in every peril of the deep; so that we all with thankful hearts may acknowledge thee, who art the Lord of the sea and of the dry land; through Jesus Christ our Lord. *Amen.*

FOR TRAVELLERS

ALMIGHTY God, who art the sure guide and strong refuge of all who put their trust in thee: We beseech thee to watch over all travellers by land or sea or air, and to vouchsafe to them thy favour and protection. Go with them where they go; dwell with them where they dwell; preserve them from all evils and dangers on their way; and of thy mercy bring them again to their homes and friends in peace; through Jesus Christ our Lord. *Amen.*

FOR THE RIGHT USE OF POSSESSIONS

LORD, who for our sakes didst become poor, though thou wast rich; to whom we owe all that we have and are, being, well-being and immortal hope: We pray thee help thy servants to make pure use of wealth and this world's good; that prodigal of our mercy we may ask for thine, and spending gladly for others may gain thee; who with the Father and the Holy Spirit dost live and reign, one God, for ever and ever. *Amen.*

LORD of all being, Maker and Master of the world and all that dwell therein: We thank thee that in thy treasure house there is ample store for the need of every child of thine. Forgive us when in our desire to possess and to enjoy, we seek for our own more than our well-earned share of this world's goods. Teach us that no man liveth to himself. May we hold all that we have as a trust to be used for the furtherance of thy kingdom in Jesus Christ. *Amen.*

FOR THE RELATIONS OF MEN TO ONE ANOTHER

O GOD, the Father of all mankind, we beseech thee to inspire us with such love, truth, and equity, that in all our dealings one with another we may shew forth our brotherhood in thee; for the sake of Jesus Christ our Lord. *Amen.*

O GOD, the King of righteousness, lead us, we pray thee, in the ways of justice and of peace: inspire us to break down all oppression and wrong, to gain for every man his due reward, and from every man his due service; that each may live for all, and all may care for each, in the name of Jesus Christ our Lord. *Amen.*

O GOD, who hast ordained that men should live and work together as brethren: Remove, we humbly beseech thee, from those who are now at variance, all spirit of strife and all occasion of bitterness; that, seeking only what is just and equal, they may ever continue in brotherly union and concord, to their own well-being, and the prosperity of the realm; through Jesus Christ our Lord. *Amen.*

FOR THE BROTHERHOOD OF MAN AND THE COUNCILS OF THE NATIONS

ALMIGHTY God, from whom all thoughts of truth and peace proceed: Kindle, we pray thee, in the hearts of all men the true love of peace, and guide with thy pure and peaceable wisdom those who take counsel for the nations of the earth; that in tranquillity thy kingdom may go forward, till the earth is filled with the knowledge of thy love; through Jesus Christ our Lord. *Amen.*

O GOD, our Father, increase in every nation the sense of human brotherhood, true respect for man and for woman, loyalty in service and charity, happiness in work and justice in reward; that our homes may be kept safe and pure, our cities renewed in beauty and order, and all the world may reflect the radiance of thy throne in heaven; through Jesus Christ our Lord. *Amen.*

O GOD, who hast made man in thine own likeness, and who dost love all whom thou hast made: Teach us the unity of thy family and the breadth of thy love. By the example of thy Son, Jesus our Saviour, enable us, while loving and serving our own, to enter into the fellowship of the whole human family; and forbid that, from pride of race or hardness of heart, we should despise any for whom Christ died, or injure any in whom he lives; for his name's sake. *Amen.*

O ETERNAL God, in whose will is our peace: We commend unto thee the needs of all the world: where there is hatred, give love; where there is injury, pardon; where there is doubt, faith; where there is despair, hope; where there is darkness, light; where there is sadness, joy; for thy mercy and thy truth's sake. *Amen.*

FOR THOSE IN DISTRESS

O THOU who art love, and who seest all the suffering, injustice, and misery which reign in this world: Have pity, we implore thee, on the work of thy hands. Look mercifully upon the poor, the oppressed, and all who are heavy laden with error, labour, or sorrow. Fill our hearts with deep compassion for those who suffer, and hasten the coming of thy kingdom of justice and truth; for the sake of Jesus Christ our Lord. *Amen.*

BLESSED Lord, who for our sakes wast content to bear sorrow and want and death: Grant unto us such a measure of thy Spirit that we may follow thee in all thy courage and self-denial, and help us by thy great love, to succour the afflicted, to relieve the needy and destitute, to share the burdens of the heavy laden and to see thee in all who are poor and desolate; who livest and reignest with the Father and the Holy Spirit, one God, world without end. *Amen.*

ALMIGHTY Father, who in thy Word hast taught us that no man lives or dies unto himself: Grant us so to fulfil the law of Christ that in bearing one another's burdens we may share in thy work of redemption; through him who has borne our infirmities, and now liveth and reigneth, world without end. *Amen.*

ALMIGHTY and everlasting God, the comfort of the sad, the strength of them that suffer: Let the prayers of thy children who cry out of any tribulation come unto thee, that all may rejoice to find that thy mercy is present with them in their affliction; through Jesus Christ our Lord. *Amen.*

FOR THE SICK

ALMIGHTY Father, giver of life and health: Look mercifully, we beseech thee, on the sick and suffering, especially those for whom our prayers are desired, that by thy blessing upon them and upon those who minister to them, they may be restored, if it be thy gracious will, to health of body and mind, and give thanks to thee in thy holy Church; through Jesus Christ our Lord. *Amen.*

FOR HOSPITALS, PHYSICIANS, NURSES

ALMIGHTY God, whose blessed Son Jesus Christ went about continually doing good, and healing all manner of sickness and all manner of disease among the people: Continue, we beseech thee, this his gracious work among us, especially in the Hospitals of our land; cheer, heal, and sanctify the sick; grant to the physicians, surgeons, and nurses wisdom and skill, sympathy and patience; and send down thy blessing on all who labour to prevent suffering and to forward thy purposes of love; through Jesus Christ our Lord. *Amen.*

FOR THE DYING

ALMIGHTY God, with whom do live the spirits of just men made perfect: We humbly commend the soul of this thy servant into the hands of a faithful Creator and merciful Saviour. Wash *him*, we pray thee, in the blood of the Lamb that was slain to take away the sin of the world, that, every defilement being purged and done away, *he* may be presented pure and spotless before thee; through the merits of Jesus Christ our Lord. *Amen.*

HEAVENLY Father, whose Son Jesus Christ did take little children into his arms and bless them, and did teach us that their angels do always behold thy face: To thy loving care we commend this little child. We thank thee that thou didst give *him* to us, and cause our hearts to love *him*. Grant us to know, in our sorrow, that thou wilt gather *him* with the lambs into thy bosom; and so keep us in thy faith and fear that, together with *him*, we may obtain the fulness of thy promises in the world to come; through Jesus Christ our Lord. *Amen.*

THE LIFE IN CHRIST: FRUITS OF THE SPIRIT

O GOD, who hast given unto us thy Son to be an example and a help to our weakness in following the path that leadeth unto life: Grant us so to be his disciples that we may tread in his footsteps; for his name's sake. *Amen.*

O MERCIFUL God, fill our hearts, we pray thee, with the graces of thy Holy Spirit, with love, joy, peace, longsuffering, gentleness, goodness, faith, meekness, temperance. Teach us to love those who hate us, to pray for those who despitefully use us, that we may be the children of thee our Father, who makest thy sun to shine on the evil and on the good, and sendest rain on the just and on the unjust. In adversity grant us grace to be patient; in prosperity keep us humble; may we guard the door of our lips; may we lightly esteem the pleasures of this world, and thirst after heavenly things; through Jesus Christ our Lord. *Amen.*

GIVE us, O Lord, purity of lips, clean and innocent hearts, and rectitude of action; give us humility, patience, self-control, prudence, justice, and courage; give us the spirit of wisdom and understanding, the spirit of counsel and strength, the spirit of knowledge and godliness, and of thy fear; make us ever to seek thy face with all our heart, all our soul, all our mind; grant us to have a contrite and humbled heart in thy presence, to prefer nothing to thy love. Have mercy upon us, we humbly beseech thee; through Jesus Christ our Lord. *Amen.*

HEAR our prayers, O Lord, and consider our desires. Give unto us true humility, a meek and quiet spirit, a loving and a friendly, a holy and a useful manner of life; bearing the burdens of our neighbours, denying ourselves, and studying to benefit others, and to please thee in all things. Grant us to be righteous in performing promises, loving to our relatives, careful of our charges; to be gentle and easy to be entreated, slow to anger, and readily prepared for every good work; through Jesus Christ our Lord. *Amen.*

LOOK upon us, O Lord, and let all the darkness of our souls vanish before the beams of thy brightness. Fill us with holy love, and open to us the treasures of thy wisdom. All our desire is known unto thee, therefore perfect what thou hast begun, and what thy Spirit has awakened us to ask in prayer. We seek thy face; turn thy face unto us and show us thy glory. Then shall our longing be satisfied, and our peace shall be perfect; through Jesus Christ our Lord. *Amen.*

ALMIGHTY and everlasting God, in whom we live and move and have our being, who hast created us for thyself so that we can find rest only in thee: Grant unto us purity of heart and strength of purpose, so that no selfish passion may hinder us from knowing thy will, and no weakness from doing it; that in thy light we may see light clearly, and in thy service find perfect freedom; through the Spirit of Jesus Christ. *Amen.*

FOR SURRENDER OF WILL

LORD, we know not what we ought to ask of thee; thou only knowest what we need; thou lovest us better than we know how to love ourselves. O Father, give to us, thy children, that which we ourselves know not how to ask. We would have no other desire than to accomplish thy will. Teach us to pray. Pray thyself in us for Christ's sake. *Amen.*

O OUR God, bestow upon us such confidence, such peace, such happiness in thee, that thy will may always be dearer to us than our own will, and thy pleasure than our own pleasure. All that thou givest is thy free gift to us, all that thou takest away is thy grace to us. Be thou thanked for all, praised for all, loved for all; through Jesus Christ our Lord. *Amen.*

FOR GUIDANCE AND PROTECTION

O GOD, by whom the meek are guided in judgment and light riseth up in darkness for the godly: Grant us, in our doubts and uncertainties, the grace to ask what thou wouldest have us to do; that the Spirit of wisdom may save us from false choices, and that in thy light we may see light, and in thy straight path may not stumble; through Jesus Christ our Lord. *Amen.*

O THOU Maker and Preserver of all things, visible and invisible: Keep, we beseech thee, the work of thine own hands, who trust in thy mercy alone for safety and protection. Guard us with the power of thy grace, here and in all places, now and at all times for evermore; through Jesus Christ our Lord. *Amen.*

O GOD, Lord of all power and might, Preserver of all thy creatures: Keep us this day in health of body and soundness of mind, in purity of heart and cheerfulness of spirit, in contentment with our lot and charity with our neighbour; and further all our lawful undertakings with thy blessing. In our labour strengthen us: in our pleasure purify us: in our difficulties direct us: in our perils defend us: in our troubles comfort us: and supply all our needs, according to the riches of thy grace in Christ Jesus our Lord. *Amen.*

FOR DIVINE STRENGTH

ALMIGHTY and merciful God, who dost grant unto thy faithful people the grace to make every path of life temporal, the strait and narrow way which leadeth unto life eternal: Grant that we, who know that we have no strength as of ourselves to help ourselves, and therefore do put all our trust in thine almighty power, may, by the assistance of thy heavenly grace, always prevail in all things against whatsoever shall arise to fight against us; through Jesus Christ our Lord. *Amen.*

O LORD, give us all, we beseech thee, grace and strength to overcome every sin; sins of besetment, deliberation, surprise, negligence, omission; sins against thee, our self, our neighbour; sins great, small, remembered, forgotten; through Jesus Christ our Lord. *Amen.*

FOR LOVE TOWARD GOD

O GOD, who hast prepared for them that love thee such good things as pass man's understanding: Pour into our hearts such love towards thee, that we, loving thee above all things, may obtain thy promises, which exceed all we can desire; through Jesus Christ our Lord. *Amen.*

O GOD, the God of all goodness and of all grace, who art worthy of a greater love than we can either give or understand: Fill our hearts, we beseech thee, with such love towards thee that nothing may seem too hard for us to do or to suffer in obedience to thy will; and grant that thus loving thee, we may become daily more like unto thee, and finally obtain the crown of life which thou hast promised to those that love thee; through Jesus Christ our Lord. *Amen.*

O LORD our God, grant us grace to desire thee with our whole heart, that so desiring, we may seek and find thee; and so finding thee, we may love thee; and loving thee we may hate those sins from which thou hast redeemed us; for the sake of Jesus Christ. *Amen.*

FOR BROTHERLY LOVE

O GOD of love, who hast given a new commandment, through thine only-begotten Son, that we should love one another even as thou didst love us, the unworthy and the wandering, and gavest thy beloved Son for our life and salvation: We pray thee, Lord, give to thy servants, in all time of our life on earth, a mind forgetful of past ill-will, a pure conscience and sincere thoughts, and a heart to love our brethren; through Jesus Christ our Lord. *Amen.*

O GOD, fountain of love, pour thy love into our souls that we may love those whom thou lovest with the love thou givest us, and think and speak of them tenderly, meekly, lovingly; and so loving our brethren and sisters for thy sake, may grow in thy love, and dwelling in love may dwell in thee; for Jesus Christ's sake. *Amen.*

FOR SINCERITY

ALMIGHTY God, who hast sent the Spirit of truth unto us to guide us into all truth: So rule our lives by thy power, that we may be truthful in word, deed, and thought. O keep us, most merciful Saviour, with thy gracious protection, that no fear or hope may ever make us false in act or speech. Cast out from us whatsoever loveth or maketh a lie, and bring us all to the perfect freedom of thy truth; through Jesus Christ, thy Son, our Lord. *Amen.*

FOR ZEAL

O GOD, the sovereign good of the soul, who requirest the hearts of all thy children: Deliver us from all sloth in thy work, all coldness in thy cause; and grant us by looking unto thee to rekindle our love, and by waiting upon thee to renew our strength; through Jesus Christ our Lord. *Amen.*

FOR LOYALTY

TEACH us, good Lord, to serve thee as thou deservest; to give and not to count the cost; to fight and not to heed the wounds; to toil and not to seek for rest; to labour and not to ask for any reward, save that of knowing that we do thy will; through the same Jesus Christ our Lord. *Amen.*

FOR PEACE

O GOD, from whom all holy desires, all good counsels, and all just works do proceed: Give unto thy servants that peace which the world cannot give; that both our hearts may be set to obey thy commandments, and also that by thee we being defended from the fear of our enemies may pass our time in rest and quietness; through the merits of Jesus Christ our Saviour. *Amen.*

O GOD, who art the author of peace and lover of concord, in knowledge of whom standeth our eternal life, whose service is perfect freedom: Defend us thy humble servants in all assaults of our enemies; that we, surely trusting in thy defence, may not fear the power of any adversaries, through the might of Jesus Christ our Lord. *Amen.*

GRANT unto us, O heavenly Father, thy peace that passeth understanding, that we, amid the storms and troubles of this our life, may rest in thee, knowing that all things are in thee, under thy care, governed by thy will, guarded by thy love; so that with a quiet heart we may face the storms of life, the cloud and the thick darkness; ever rejoicing to know that the darkness and the light are both alike to thee; through Jesus Christ our Lord. *Amen.*

LET us not seek out of thee what we can find only in thee, O Lord, peace and rest, and joy and bliss, which abide only in thine abiding joy. Lift up our souls above the weary round of harassing thoughts to thy eternal presence. Lift up our souls to the pure, bright, serene, radiant atmosphere of thy presence, that there we may breathe freely, there repose in thy love, there be at rest from ourselves and from all things that weary us, and thence return arrayed with thy peace to do and bear what shall please thee; for the sake of Jesus Christ our Lord. *Amen.*

O LORD God, who art the shadow of a great rock in a weary land, who beholdest thy weak creatures, weary of labour, weary of pleasure, weary of hope deferred, weary of self, in thine abundant compassion and unutterable tenderness: Bring us, we pray thee, unto thy rest; through Jesus Christ, thy Son, our Lord. *Amen.*

FOR ILLUMINATION

LORD God, who art from everlasting to everlasting: To thee we bring the wants which none but thyself can satisfy, and the unquiet hearts which thou alone canst still.

We dwell in the changing light and darkness of this world, but thou dwellest ever in the light. Have mercy upon us when we are blind to thy glory and forgetful of thy truth; when we refuse to be guided by thy Spirit and trust in ourselves alone. From the darkness of our ways lead us to thy light, and grant us the knowledge of thy forgiveness; through Jesus Christ our Lord. *Amen.*

FOR COURAGE

GOD of our life: Help us in the days when the burdens we carry chafe our shoulders and weigh us down: when the road seems dreary and endless, the skies grey and threatening; when our lives have no music in them, our hearts are lonely, and our souls have lost their courage. Flood the path with light, we beseech thee; turn our eyes to where the skies are full of promise; tune our hearts to brave music; bind us in comradeship with the heroes and saints of every age; and so quicken our spirits that we may be able to encourage the souls of all who journey with us on the road of life; to thy honour and glory. *Amen.*

IN THE MORNING

O LORD, our heavenly Father, Almighty and everlasting God, who hast safely brought us to the beginning of this day: Defend us in the same with thy mighty power; and grant that this day we fall into no sin, neither run into any kind of danger; but that all our doings may be ordered by thy governance, to do always that is righteous in thy sight; through Jesus Christ our Lord. *Amen.*

INTO thy hands, O Lord, we commit ourselves this day. Give to each one of us a watchful, a humble, and a diligent spirit, that we may seek in all things to know thy will, and when we know it may perform it perfectly and gladly, to the honour and glory of thy name; through Jesus Christ our Lord. *Amen.*

GRANT us, O Lord, to pass this day in gladness and peace, without stumbling and without stain; that reaching the eventide victorious over all temptation, we may praise thee, the eternal God, who art blessed, and dost govern all things, world without end. *Amen.*

OUR heavenly Father, we thank thee for the summons of a new day. As we wait on thee, we pray that thou wouldst fill our minds with thy truth, our hearts with thy love, our wills with thy peace, and our lives with thy strength; through Jesus Christ our Lord. *Amen.*

ALMIGHTY God, our Father and Preserver: We give thee thanks that of thy goodness thou hast watched over us the past night, and brought us to a new day; and we beseech thee to strengthen and guard us by thy Spirit, that we may spend it wholly in thy service, and to thy glory, looking for all prosperity to thy blessing, and seeking only those things which are well-pleasing in thy sight. Enable us, O Lord, while we labour for the life that now is, ever to have regard unto that heavenly life which thou hast promised thy children. Defend us in soul and body from all harm. And seeing it is a small thing to have begun well, except we also persevere, take us, O Lord, into thy good keeping this day and all our days: continue and increase thy grace within us, until we shall be perfectly united in the glory of thy Son; through Jesus Christ our Lord. *Amen.*

WE give thee thanks, Lord God of our salvation, because thou doest all things for the good of our life, that we may always look steadfastly unto thee, the Saviour and Benefactor of our souls, for thou hast refreshed us in the night past, and raised us up, and brought us to worship thy glorious name. Wherefore, we beseech thee, O Lord, give us grace and power, that we may be accounted worthy to sing praise to thee with understanding, and to pray to thee without ceasing, in fear and trembling working out our own salvation; through Jesus Christ our Lord. *Amen.*

IN THE EVENING

LIGHTEN our darkness, we beseech thee, O Lord; and by thy great mercy defend us from all perils and dangers of this night; for the love of thy only Son, our Saviour, Jesus Christ. *Amen.*

WATCH thou, dear Lord, with those who wake, or watch, or weep to-night, and give thine angels charge over those who sleep. Tend thy sick ones, O Lord Christ. Rest thy weary ones. Bless the dying ones. Soothe the suffering ones. Pity thine afflicted ones. Shield thy joyous ones. And all, for thy love's sake. *Amen.*

O LORD our God, who dost watch over all thy creatures and hast made the night for man to rest in as thou hast ordained the day for toil: Grant that we may so take our bodily rest, that we may set our minds upon thee, love thee, fear thee, and rest in thee; furthermore, that our sleep be not excessive, but only sufficient to revive our weak nature, that so we may be the better prepared to live a godly life to the glory of thy holy name; through Jesus Christ our Lord. *Amen.*

HEAVENLY Father, who slumberest not nor sleepest: We commend to thy gracious care and keeping ourselves and all who belong to us. We thank thee for the bright and healing light of this day, and now for the restful night. Lift from our minds the burdens of our wakeful hours: visit our bodies with refreshing sleep. Through the darkness keep us safe and undefiled. And wake us to meet to-morrow's duties in strength of body and vigour of mind, with peace in our spirits and courage in our hearts; through the grace of our Lord Jesus Christ. *Amen.*

O GOD most merciful, light eternal in the darkness shining, by whom the night of sin and the blindness of our hearts are driven away: Since thou hast appointed the day for labour and the night for rest, grant unto us, we beseech thee, that our bodies may repose in peace and quietness, that afterward they may be able to endure the toil which thou hast laid upon us in thy service. Temper our sleep that it be not disorderly, and keep us spotless both in body and in soul, that our very rest may be to thy glory, renewing the strength of our hearts and our joy in thee; through Jesus Christ our Lord. *Amen.*

BEFORE ANY UNDERTAKING

PREVENT us (*or,* Go before us), O Lord, in all our doings, with thy most gracious favour, and further us with thy continual help; that in all our works, begun, continued, and ended in thee, we may glorify thy holy name, and finally by thy mercy obtain everlasting life; through Jesus Christ our Lord. *Amen.*

AT THE NEW YEAR

O THOU who art from everlasting to everlasting, replenish us with heavenly grace, at the beginning of this year, that we may be enabled to accept all its duties, to perform all its labours, to welcome all its mercies, to meet all its trials, and to advance through all it holds in store for us, with cheerful courage and a constant mind. O Lord, suffer us not to be separated from thee, either by joy or sorrow, or any sin or weakness of our own; but have compassion upon us, and forgive us, and keep us in the strong confidence of thine eternal love in Jesus Christ: that as thou hast called us to immortality through him, so we may pass the residue of our years in the power of an endless life; and to thy name shall be all the praise. *Amen.*

O ETERNAL God, who makest all things new, and abidest for ever the same: Grant us to begin this year in thy faith, and to continue it in thy favour; that, being guided in all our doings, and guarded all our days, we may spend our lives in thy service, and finally, by thy grace, attain the glory of everlasting life; through Jesus Christ our Lord. *Amen.*

ALMIGHTY and eternal God, with whom one day is as a thousand years, and a thousand years as one day: We bring thee thanks and praise for thy blessings more than we can number with which thou hast crowned our lives during the year now past; and since thy mercies are ever new, let the new year which has now begun be to us a year of grace and of salvation. Have pity upon us in our frailty, whose days are as the grass; and establish us in the fellowship of that life which is the same yesterday and to-day and for ever. Graciously protect and conduct us through the uncertainties of this new year of our earthly pilgrimage; prepare us for its duties, its trials, its joys, and its sorrows; and grant that every change that it brings with it, whether of life or death, may bring us nearer to thee, and nearer to the great eternal year of rest and joy, which awaits the faithful in thy blessed presence; through Jesus Christ our Lord. *Amen.*

PRAYERS WHICH MAY BE SAID AFTER ANY OF THE FORMER

REMEMBER, O Lord, what thou hast wrought in us, and not what we deserve; and as thou hast called us to thy service, make us worthy of our calling; through Jesus Christ our Lord. *Amen.*

GRANT us, O Lord, not to mind earthly things, but to love things heavenly; and even now, while we are placed among things that are passing away, to cleave to those that shall abide; through Jesus Christ our Lord. *Amen.*

O LORD, we beseech thee mercifully to receive the prayers of thy people who call upon thee; and grant that they may both perceive and know what things they ought to do, and also may have grace and power faithfully to fulfil the same; through Jesus Christ our Lord. *Amen.*

ASCRIPTIONS OF GLORY

Now unto him that is able to do exceeding abundantly above all that we ask or think, according to the power that worketh in us; unto him be glory in the Church by Christ Jesus, throughout all ages, world without end. *Amen.*

Now unto the God of all grace, who hath called us unto his eternal glory by Christ Jesus, be glory and dominion for ever and ever. *Amen.*

Now unto the King eternal, immortal, invisible, the only wise God, be honour and glory for ever and ever. *Amen.*

Unto him that loveth us, and loosed us from our sins in his own blood, and hath made us a kingdom and priests unto God and his Father; to him be glory and dominion for ever and ever. *Amen.*

Now unto him that is able to keep you from falling, and to present you faultless before the presence of his glory with exceeding joy: to the only wise God our Saviour, be glory and majesty, dominion and power, both now and ever. *Amen.*

Unto the Father, and unto the Son, and unto the Holy Spirit, be ascribed in the Church all honour and glory, might, majesty, dominion, and blessing, now, henceforth, and for ever. *Amen.*

Blessing, and honour, and glory, and power, be unto him that sitteth upon the throne, and unto the Lamb, for ever and ever. *Amen.*

Worthy is the Lamb that was slain to receive power, and riches, and wisdom, and strength, and honour, and glory, and blessing. *Amen.*

Salvation unto our God which sitteth upon the throne, and unto the Lamb. *Amen.*

Blessing, and glory, and wisdom, and thanksgiving, and honour, and power, and might, be unto our God for ever and ever. *Amen.*

Great and marvellous are thy works, Lord God Almighty; just and true are thy ways, thou King of saints. Who shall not fear thee and glorify thy name, for thou only art holy? *Amen.*

Salvation, and glory, and honour, and power unto the Lord our God. *Amen.*

Hallelujah! for the Lord God Omnipotent reigneth. KING OF KINGS, AND LORD OF LORDS. *Amen.*

A TABLE OF LESSONS

WITH PRAYERS FOR GRACE

¶ *These Lessons may be used with either the first or the second Directory for Public Worship, or with the Order for the Lord's Supper. The Prayers for Grace may be used with the second Directory or with the Order for the Lord's Supper.*

¶ *When three Lessons are set down, all three may be used, or the first and the third, or the second and the third, or even the third alone.*

THE SEASON OF ADVENT

(The four Sundays before Christmas)

In the last weeks before Christmas the Church prepares to celebrate the Coming of the Lord Christ. It is a time of penitence and humble expectancy.

I

ALMIGHTY God, give us grace that we may cast away the works of darkness, and put upon us the armour of light, now in the time of this mortal life, in which thy Son Jesus Christ came to visit us in great humility; that in the last day, when he shall come again in his glorious Majesty to judge both the quick and the dead, we may rise to the life immortal; through him who liveth and reigneth with thee and the Holy Spirit, now and ever. *Amen.*

Isaiah 60. 1-11.

Romans 13. 8-14.

St. Matthew 21. 1-9, *or* 21. 1-13.

II

BLESSED Lord, who hast caused all holy Scriptures to be written for our learning: Grant that we may in such wise hear them, read, mark, learn, and inwardly digest them, that by patience, and comfort of thy holy Word, we may embrace, and ever hold fast the blessed hope of everlasting life, which thou hast given us in our Saviour Jesus Christ. *Amen.*

Isaiah 35, *or* 32. 1-4, 16-18.

Romans 15. 4-13.

St. Luke 21. 25-31, *or* St. Matthew 25. 1-13.

III

O LORD Jesus Christ, who at thy first coming didst send thy messenger to prepare thy way before thee: Grant that the ministers and stewards of thy mysteries may likewise so prepare and make ready thy way, by turning the hearts of the disobedient to the wisdom of the just, that at thy second coming to judge the world we may be found an acceptable people in thy sight; who livest and reignest with the Father and the Holy Spirit, ever one God, world without end. *Amen.*

Isaiah 62. 10-12.

1 Corinthians 4. 1-5.

St. Matthew 11. 2-15.

IV

O LORD, raise up (we pray thee) thy power and come among us, and with great might succour us; that whereas, through our sins and wickedness, we are sore let and hindered in running the race that is set before us, thy bountiful grace and mercy may speedily help and deliver us; through the satisfaction of thy Son our Lord; to whom with thee and the Holy Spirit be honour and glory, world without end. *Amen.*

Isaiah 40. 1-11.

Philippians 4. 4-7.

St. John 1. 19-28, *or* St. Luke 3. 3-14.

THE SEASON OF CHRISTMAS

(From December 25 to January 5)

At this time the Church remembers that her Lord became man for us men and our salvation.

I

O GOD, who makest us glad with the yearly remembrance of the birth of thy only Son Jesus Christ: Grant that as we joyfully receive him for our Redeemer, so we may with sure confidence behold him when he shall come to be our Judge; who liveth and reigneth with thee and the Holy Spirit, one God, world without end. *Amen.*

Or this.

MERCIFUL and most loving God, by whose will and bountiful gift Jesus Christ our Lord humbled himself that he might exalt mankind; and became flesh that he might renew in us the divine image: Grant unto us the inheritance of the meek, perfect in us thy likeness, and bring us at last to rejoice in beholding thy beauty, and, with all thy saints, to glorify thy grace, who hast given thine only-begotten Son to be the Saviour of the world. *Amen.*

Micah 4. 2, 4, 5a.
Titus 2. 11-14.
St. Luke 2. 1-14.

II

ALMIGHTY God, who didst wonderfully create man in thine own image, and didst yet more wonderfully restore him: Grant, we beseech thee, that as thy Son our Lord Jesus Christ was made in the likeness of men, so we may be made partakers of the divine nature; through the same thy Son, who with thee and the Holy Spirit liveth and reigneth, one God, world without end. *Amen.*

Isaiah 9. 2-7, *or* 11. 1-9.
Hebrews 1. 1-12, *or* 2 Corinthians 8. 9.
St. John 1. 1-14.

THE SEASON OF EPIPHANY

(From January 6 till the beginning of Lent)

At this time the Church remembers that the true light hath shone forth to the ends of the earth.

I

O GOD, who by the leading of a star didst manifest thy only begotten Son to the Gentiles: Mercifuly grant that we, which know thee now by faith, may at length come to behold the beauty of thy Majesty; through Jesus Christ our Lord. *Amen.*

Isaiah 60. 1-6.
Ephesians 3. 1-12.
St. Matthew 2. 1-12.

II

O GOD, whose blessed Son was manifested that he might fulfil all righteousness, and make us the sons of God, and heirs of eternal life: Grant us, we beseech thee, that having this hope, we may purify ourselves, even as he is pure; that, when he shall appear again with power and great glory, we may be made like unto him in his eternal and glorious kingdom; where with thee, O Father, and thee, O Holy Spirit, he liveth and reigneth, ever one God, world without end. *Amen.*

Micah 4. 1-4.
Ephesians 2. 11-18.
St. Luke 2. 25-35.

III

O LORD, we beseech thee mercifully to receive the prayers of thy people which call upon thee; and grant that they may both perceive and know what things they ought to do, and also may have grace and power faithfully to fulfil the same; through Jesus Christ our Lord. *Amen.*

Romans 12. 1-5.

St. Luke 2. 41-52.

IV

ALMIGHTY and everlasting God, who dost govern all things in heaven and earth: Mercifully hear the supplications of thy people, and grant us thy peace all the days of our life; through Jesus Christ our Lord. *Amen.*

Romans 12. 6-16a.

St. John 2. 1-11.

V

ALMIGHTY and everlasting God, mercifully look upon our infirmities, and in all our dangers and necessities stretch forth thy right hand to help and defend us; through Jesus Christ our Lord. *Amen.*

Romans 12. 16b-21.

St. Matthew 8. 1-13.

VI

O GOD, who knowest us to be set in the midst of so many and great dangers, that by reason of the frailty of our nature we cannot always stand upright: Grant to us such strength and protection, as may support us in all dangers, and carry us through all temptations; through Jesus Christ our Lord. *Amen.*

Romans 13. 8-10.

St. Matthew 8. 23-27.

VII

O LORD, we beseech thee to keep thy Church and household continually in thy true religion; that they who do lean only upon the hope of thy heavenly grace may evermore be defended by thy mighty power; through Jesus Christ our Lord. *Amen.*

Colossians 3. 12-17.

St. Matthew 13. 24-30.

THE SEASON OF LENT

During these weeks the Church enters with her Lord deeper and deeper into the shadows of human sin and sorrow, that she may know the fellowship of his sufferings.

I

O LORD, we beseech thee favourably to hear the prayers of thy people; that we, who are justly afflicted for our offences, may be mercifully delivered by thy goodness, for the glory of thy name; through Jesus Christ our Saviour, who liveth and reigneth with thee and the Holy Spirit, ever one God, world without end. *Amen.*

1 Corinthians 9. 24-27.

St. Matthew 20. 1-16.

II

O LORD God, who seest that we put not our trust in any thing that we do: Mercifully grant that by thy power we may be defended against all adversity; through Jesus Christ our Lord. *Amen.*

2 Corinthians 11. 19-31.

St. Luke 8. 4-15.

III

O LORD, who has taught us that all our doings without charity are nothing worth: Send thy Holy Spirit, and pour into our hearts that most excellent gift of charity, the very bond of peace and of all virtues, without which whosoever liveth is counted dead before thee: Grant this for thine only Son Jesus Christ's sake. *Amen.*

1 Corinthians 13: 1-13.

St. Luke 18. 31-43.

IV

ALMIGHTY and everlasting God, who hatest nothing that thou hast made, and dost forgive the sins of all them that are penitent: Create and make in us new and contrite hearts, that we, worthily lamenting our sins, and acknowledging our wretchedness, may obtain of thee, the God of all mercy, perfect remission and forgiveness; through Jesus Christ our Lord. *Amen.*

Joel 2. 12-19.

St. Matthew 6. 16-21.

V

O LORD, who for our sake didst fast forty days and forty nights: Give us grace to use such abstinence, that, our flesh being subdued to the spirit, we may ever obey thy godly motions in righteousness, and true holiness, to thy honour and glory; who livest and reignest with the Father and the Holy Spirit, one God, world without end. *Amen.*

2 Corinthians 6. 1-10.

St. Matthew 4. 1-11.

VI

ALMIGHTY God, who seest that we have no power of ourselves to help ourselves: Keep us both outwardly in our bodies, and inwardly in our souls; that we may be defended from all adversities which may happen to the body, and from all evil thoughts which may assault and hurt the soul; through Jesus Christ our Lord. *Amen.*

1 Thessalonians 4. 1-8.

St. Matthew 15. 21-28.

VII

WE beseech thee, Almighty God, look upon the hearty desires of thy humble servants, and stretch forth the right hand of thy Majesty, to be our defence against all our enemies; through Jesus Christ our Lord. *Amen.*

Ephesians 5. 1-14.

St. Luke 11. 14-28.

VIII

GRANT, we beseech thee, Almighty God, that we, who for our evil deeds do worthily deserve to be punished, by the comfort of thy grace may mercifully be relieved; through our Lord and Saviour Jesus Christ. *Amen.*

Hebrews 12. 22-24.

St. John 6. 1-14

THE SUNDAY NEXT BEFORE EASTER

On this day our Lord entered into the city, going among those who were presently to bring him to the Cross. From this day till Good Friday the eyes of the Church are fastened on the Cross of her Lord.

ALMIGHTY and everlasting God, who, of thy tender love towards mankind, hast sent thy Son, our Saviour Jesus Christ, to take upon him our flesh, and to suffer death upon the Cross, that all mankind should follow the example of his great humility: Mercifully grant, that we may both follow the example of his patience, and also be made partakers of his resurrection; through the same Jesus Christ our Lord. *Amen.*

Philippians 2. 5-11.

St. Matthew 26. 1 to 27. 61, *or* 27. 1-54, *or* 21. 1-9.

THE MONDAY BEFORE EASTER

ALMIGHTY and everlasting God, who, of thy tender love towards mankind, hast sent thy Son, our Saviour Jesus Christ, to take upon him our flesh, and to suffer death upon the Cross, that all mankind should follow the example of his great humility: Mercifully grant, that we may both follow the example of his patience, and also be made partakers of his resurrection; through the same Jesus Christ our Lord. *Amen.*

Isaiah 63. 7-16.

Romans 5. 1-8.

St. Mark 14, *or* St. John 12. 1-11.

THE TUESDAY BEFORE EASTER

ALMIGHTY and everlasting God, who, of thy tender love towards mankind, hast sent thy Son, our Saviour Jesus Christ, to take upon him our flesh, and to suffer death upon the Cross, that all mankind should follow the example of his great humility: Mercifully grant, that we may both follow the example of his patience, and also be made partakers of his resurrection; through the same Jesus Christ our Lord. *Amen.*

Isaiah 50. 5-10.

Ephesians 2. 13-22.

St. Mark 15, *or* 15. 1-39.

THE WEDNESDAY BEFORE EASTER

ALMIGHTY and everlasting God, who, of thy tender love towards mankind, hast sent thy Son, our Saviour Jesus Christ, to take upon him our flesh, and to suffer death upon the Cross, that all mankind should follow the example of his great humility: Mercifully grant, that we may both follow the example of his patience, and also be made partakers of his resurrection; through the same Jesus Christ our Lord. *Amen.*

Isaiah 62. 11 to 63. 1.

1 St. John 4. 7-11.

St. Luke 22.

THE THURSDAY BEFORE EASTER

I

BE present, O Lord, unto us, we beseech thee, and as thou gavest us an example by washing the feet of thy disciples and wiping them free from all outward defilement, so grant us grace ever to serve one another in true humility, and do thou vouchsafe that we may have the inward defilement of all our sins made clean by thee; who livest and reignest with the Father in the unity of the Holy Spirit, one God, world without end. *Amen.*

1 St. John 4. 7-19.

St. Luke 23, *or* 23. 1-47, *or* St. John 13. 1-15.

II

O LORD Jesus Christ, who hast ordained this holy Sacrament to be a pledge of thy love, and a continual remembrance of thy passion: Grant that we, who partake thereof by faith with thanksgiving, may grow up into thee in all things, until we come to thy eternal joy; who with the Father and the Holy Spirit livest and reignest, one God, world without end. *Amen.*

1 Corinthians 11. 23-28.

St. John 6. 53-63.

GOOD FRIDAY

ALMIGHTY God, we beseech thee graciously to behold this thy family, for which our Lord Jesus Christ was content to be betrayed, and given up into the hands of wicked men, and to suffer death upon the Cross; who now liveth and reigneth with thee and the Holy Spirit, ever one God, world without end. *Amen.*

ALMIGHTY and everlasting God, by whose Spirit the whole body of the Church is governed and sanctified: Receive our supplications and prayers, which we offer before thee for all estates of men in thy holy Church, that every member of the same, in his vocation and ministry, may truly and godly serve thee; through our Lord and Saviour Jesus Christ. *Amen.*

O MERCIFUL God, who hast made all men, and hatest nothing that thou hast made, nor wouldest the death of a sinner, but rather that he should be converted and live: Have mercy upon all who have not come to the knowledge of the truth and the faith of the Gospel; take from them all ignorance, hardness of heart, and contempt of thy Word; and so fetch them home, blessed Lord, that they may be made one flock under one shepherd, Jesus Christ our Lord. *Amen.*

LORD, let the view of the Cross ever fill our souls with happy peace, with holy love, and with heavenly joy; through Jesus Christ. *Amen.*

Isaiah 53.

Hebrews 10. 4-25.

St. John 18, 19, *or* 19. 1-37.

EASTER DAY

On this day the Church remembers that her Lord overcame sin and death, and brought life and immortality to light.

I

O GOD who by thine only-begotten Son hast overcome death and opened to us the gate of everlasting life: Grant us, we beseech thee, that we who celebrate the festival of our Lord's resurrection, may by the renewing of thy Spirit arise from the death of the soul; through Jesus Christ our Lord. *Amen.*

Colossians 3. 1-11.

St. John 20. 1-10.

II

O GOD, who through the mighty resurrection of thy Son Jesus Christ from the dead, hast delivered us from the power of darkness into the kingdom of thy love: Grant, we beseech thee, that as by his death he has recalled us into life, so by his presence ever abiding in us he may raise us to joys eternal; through him who for our sakes died and rose again, and is ever with us in power and great glory, even the same Jesus Christ our Lord. *Amen.*

Revelation 1. 10-18.

St. Luke 24. 1-12.

THE SEASON OF EASTER
(From Easter Day till Pentecost)

During this time the Church, knowing in herself the power of his resurrection, rejoices in her living Lord.

I

O GOD, who for our redemption, didst give thine only-begotten Son to the death of the Cross, and by his glorious resurrection hast delivered us from the power of our enemy: Grant us so to die daily unto sin, that we may evermore live with him in the joy of his resurrection; through the same Jesus Christ our Lord. *Amen.*

Acts 10. 34-43, *or* 13. 26-33a, *or* Romans 6. 2-11.

St. Luke 24. 13-35, *or* 24. 36-49.

II

ALMIGHTY Father, who hast given thine only Son to die for our sins, and to rise again for our justification: Grant us so to put away the leaven of malice and wickedness, that we may alway serve thee in pureness of living and truth; through the merits of the same thy Son Jesus Christ our Lord. *Amen.*

1 St. John 5. 4-12.

St. John 20. 19-31.

III

ALMIGHTY God, who hast given thine only Son to be unto us both a sacrifice for sin, and also an example of godly life: Give us grace that we may always most thankfully receive his inestimable benefit, and also daily endeavour ourselves to follow the blessed steps of his most holy life; through the same Jesus Christ our Lord. *Amen.*

1 St. Peter 2. 19-25.

St. John 10. 11-16.

IV

ALMIGHTY God, who shewest to them that be in error the light of thy truth, to the intent that they may return into the way of righteousness: Grant unto all them that are admitted into the fellowship of Christ's religion, that they may eschew those things that are contrary to their profession, and follow all such things as are agreeable to the same; through our Lord Jesus Christ. *Amen.*

1 St. Peter 2. 11-17.

St. John 16. 16-22.

V

O ALMIGHTY God, who alone canst order the unruly wills and affections of sinful men: Grant unto thy people, that they may love the thing which thou commandest, and desire that which thou dost promise; that so, among the sundry and manifold changes of the world, our hearts may surely there be fixed, where true joys are to be found; through Jesus Christ our Lord. *Amen.*

St. James 1. 17-21.

St. John 16. 2-15.

VI

O LORD, from whom all good things do come: Grant to us thy humble servants, that by thy holy inspiration we may think those things that be good, and by thy merciful guiding may perform the same; through our Lord Jesus Christ. *Amen.*

St. James 1. 22-27.

St. John 16. 23-33.

VII

GRANT, we beseech thee, Almighty God, that, as thy only begotten Son our Lord Jesus Christ ascended into the heavens; so we may also in heart and mind thither ascend, and with him continually dwell, who liveth and reigneth with thee and the Holy Spirit, one God, world without end. *Amen.*

Acts 1. 1-11, *or* Revelation 5.

St. Mark 16. 14-20, *or* St. Luke 24. 44-53.

VIII

O GOD, the King of glory, who hast exalted thine only Son Jesus Christ with great triumph unto thy kingdom in heaven: We beseech thee, leave us not comfortless; but send to us thy Holy Spirit to comfort us, and exalt us unto the same place whither our Saviour Christ is gone before, who liveth and reigneth with thee and the Holy Spirit, one God, world without end. *Amen.*

1 St. Peter 4. 7-11.

St. John 15. 26 to 16. 4a.

IX

O LORD Jesus Christ, who didst gloriously ascend that thou mightest fill all things, and didst come to thy Church on earth, bringing gifts for men: So dwell with us continually on earth that we may ever be with thee in heaven; where with the Father and the Holy Spirit thou livest and reignest, one God, world without end. *Amen.*

Ephesians 4. 1-13.

St. John 14. 12-21.

PENTECOST

(Seven Weeks after Easter)

At this time the Church remembers the coming of the Spirit of Christ in his fullness.

GOD, who as at this time didst teach the hearts of thy faithful people, by the sending to them the light of thy Holy Spirit: Grant us by the same Spirit to have a right judgement in all things, and evermore to rejoice in his holy comfort; through the merits of Christ Jesus our Saviour, who liveth and reigneth with thee, in the unity of the same Spirit, one God, world without end. *Amen.*

Or this.

O ETERNAL God, the Father of spirits and the lover of souls, who didst send thy Holy Spirit upon thy Church on the day of Pentecost, and hast promised that he shall abide with it for ever: Let that same Spirit lead us into all truth, defend us from all sin, enrich us with his gifts, refresh us with his comfort, rule our hearts in all things, and lead us in the way everlasting; through Jesus

Christ our Lord, who with thee and the same Spirit, liveth and reigneth, one God, world without end. *Amen.*

Or this.

O GOD, who in the exaltation of thy Son Jesus Christ dost sanctify thy universal Church: Shed abroad in every race and nation the gift of his Spirit; that the work wrought by his power at the first preaching of the Gospel may be extended throughout the whole world; through the same our Lord Jesus Christ, who liveth and reigneth with thee in the unity of the same Spirit now and ever. *Amen.*

Joel 2. 23-32, *or* Ezekiel 37. 1-14.

Acts 2. 1-11, *or* 10. 34-48a.

St. John 3. 16-21, *or* 10. 1-10, *or* 14. 15-31 (even so I do).

THE SEASON OF PENTECOST

(From Pentecost till the beginning of Advent)

Throughout this time the Church remembers that the experience of Pentecost is to be continually renewed, the Gospel of Christ preached to all mankind, and the fruits of the Spirit matured in the lives of her members.

I

O GOD of unchangeable power and eternal light, look favourably on thy whole Church, that wonderful and sacred mystery; and, by the tranquil operation of thy perpetual providence, carry out the work of man's salvation; that things which were cast down may be raised up, and that all things may come to perfection through him by whom all things were made, even through our Lord Jesus Christ. *Amen.*

Ephesians 2. 11-22, *or* 4. 1-16.

St. Matthew 16. 13-18.

II

O GOD, the strength of all them that put their trust in thee, mercifully accept our prayers; and because through the weakness of our mortal nature we can do no good thing without thee, grant us the help of thy grace, that in keeping of thy commandments we may please thee, both in will and deed; through Jesus Christ our Lord. *Amen.*

1 St. John 4. 7-21.

St. Luke 16. 19-31.

III

O LORD, who never failest to help and govern them whom thou dost bring up in thy steadfast fear and love: Keep us, we beseech thee, under the protection of thy good providence, and make us to have a perpetual fear and love of thy holy name; through Jesus Christ our Lord. *Amen.*

1 St. John 3. 13-18.

St. Luke 14. 16-24.

IV

WE beseech thee, O Lord, to renew thy people inwardly and outwardly, that as thou wouldest not have them to be hindered by bodily pleasure, thou mayest make them vigorous with spiritual purpose, and refresh them in such sort by things transitory that thou mayest grant them rather to cleave to things eternal; through Jesus Christ our Lord. *Amen.*

1 St. Peter 5. 5-11.

St. Luke 15. 1-10.

V

O GOD, the Protector of all that trust in thee, without whom nothing is strong, nothing is holy: Increase and multiply upon us thy mercy; that, thou being our ruler and guide, we may so pass through things temporal that we finally lose not the things eternal: grant this, O heavenly Father, for Jesus Christ's sake our Lord. *Amen.*

Romans 8. 18-23.

St. Luke 6. 36-42.

VI

GRANT, O Lord, we beseech thee, that the course of this world may be so peaceably ordered by thy governance, that thy Church may joyfully serve thee in all godly quietness; through Jesus Christ our Lord. *Amen.*

1 St. Peter 3. 8-15.

St. Luke 5. 1-11.

VII

O GOD, who hast prepared for them that love thee such good things as pass man's understanding: Pour into our hearts such love towards thee, that we, loving thee above all things, may obtain thy promises, which exceed all that we can desire; through Jesus Christ our Lord. *Amen.*

Romans 6. 3-11.

St. Matthew 5. 20-26.

VIII

LORD of all power and might, who art the author and giver of all good things: Graft in our hearts the love of thy name, increase in us true religion, nourish us with all goodness, and of thy great mercy keep us in the same; through Jesus Christ our Lord. *Amen.*

Romans 6. 19-23.

St. Mark 8. 1-9.

IX

O GOD, whose never-failing providence ordereth all things both in heaven and earth: We humbly beseech thee to put away from us all hurtful things, and to give those things which be profitable for us; through Jesus Christ our Lord. *Amen.*

Romans 8. 12-17.

St. Matthew 7. 15-21.

X

GRANT to us, Lord, we beseech thee, the spirit to think and do always such things as be rightful; that we, who cannot do anything that is good without thee, may by thee be enabled to live according to thy will; through Jesus Christ our Lord. *Amen.*

1 Corinthians 10. 1-13.

St. Luke 16. 1-13, *or* 15. 11-32.

XI

LET thy merciful ears, O Lord, be open to the prayers of thy humble servants; and that they may obtain their petitions make them to ask such things as shall please thee; through Jesus Christ our Lord. *Amen.*

1 Corinthians 12. 1-11.

St. Luke 19. 41-48.

XII

O GOD, who declarest thy almighty power most chiefly in shewing mercy and pity: Mercifully grant unto us such a measure of thy grace, that we, running the way of thy commandments, may obtain thy gracious promises, and be made partakers of thy heavenly treasure; through Jesus Christ our Lord. *Amen.*

1 Corinthians 15. 1-11.

St. Luke 18. 9-14.

XIII

ALMIGHTY and everlasting God, who art always more ready to hear than we to pray, and art wont to give more than either we desire, or deserve: Pour down upon us the abundance of thy mercy; forgiving us those things whereof our conscience is afraid, and giving us those good things which we are not worthy to ask, but through the merits and mediation of Jesus Christ, thy Son, our Lord. *Amen.*

2 Corinthians 3. 4-11.

St. Mark 7. 31-37.

XIV

ALMIGHTY and merciful God, of whose only gift it cometh that thy faithful people do unto thee true and laudable service: Grant, we beseech thee, that we may so faithfully serve thee in this life, that we fail not finally to attain thy heavenly promises; through the merits of Jesus Christ our Lord. *Amen.*

Galatians 3. 16-22, *or*, Hebrews 13. 1-6.

St. Luke 10. 23-37.

XV

ALMIGHTY and everlasting God, give unto us the increase of faith, hope, and charity; and, that we may obtain that which thou dost promise, make us to love that which thou dost command; through Jesus Christ our Lord. *Amen.*

Galatians 5. 16-24.

St. Luke 17. 11-19.

XVI

KEEP, we beseech thee, O Lord, thy Church with thy perpetual mercy; and, because the frailty of man without thee cannot but fall, keep us ever by thy help from all things hurtful, and lead us to all things profitable to our salvation; through Jesus Christ our Lord. *Amen.*

Galatians 6. 11-18.

St. Matthew 6. 24-34.

XVII

O LORD, we beseech thee, let thy continual pity cleanse and defend thy Church; and, because it cannot continue in safety without thy succour, preserve it evermore by thy help and goodness: through Jesus Christ our Lord. *Amen.*

Ephesians 3. 13-21.

St. Luke 7. 11-17.

XVIII

LORD, we pray thee that thy grace may always go before and follow us, and make us continually to be given to all good works; through Jesus Christ our Lord. *Amen.*

Ephesians 4. 1-6.

St. Luke 14. 1-11.

XIX

GOD, the bestower of peace and lover of good will: Grant to thy servants to stay their minds on thee, and to live in true agreement with thy holy will; that they may be delivered from all evils that overtake them, and stand fast in all time of temptation; through Jesus Christ our Lord. *Amen.*

1 Corinthians 1. 4-9.

St. Matthew 22. 34-46.

XX

O GOD, forasmuch as without thee we are not able to please thee; mercifully grant, that thy Holy Spirit may in all things direct and rule our hearts; through Jesus Christ our Lord. *Amen.*

Ephesians 4. 17-32.

St. Matthew 9. 1-8.

XXI

ALMIGHTY and most merciful God, of thy bountiful goodness keep us, we beseech thee, from all things that may hurt us; that we, being ready both in body and soul, may cheerfully accomplish those things that thou wouldest have done; through Jesus Christ our Lord. *Amen.*

Ephesians 5. 15-21.

St. Matthew 22. 1-14.

XXII

GRANT, we beseech thee, merciful Lord, to thy faithful people pardon and peace, that they may be cleansed from all their sins, and serve thee with a quiet mind; through Jesus Christ our Lord. *Amen.*

Ephesians 6. 1-20.

St. John 4. 46b-54.

XXIII

LORD, we beseech thee to keep thy household the Church in continual godliness; that through thy protection it may be free from all adversities, and devoutly given to serve thee in good works, to the glory of thy name; through Jesus Christ our Lord. *Amen.*

Philippians 1. 3-11.

St. Matthew 18. 21-35.

XXIV

O GOD, our refuge and strength, who art the author of all godliness: Be ready, we beseech thee, to hear the devout prayers of thy Church; and grant that those things which we ask faithfully we may obtain effectually; through Jesus Christ our Lord. *Amen.*

Philippians 3. 17-21.

St. Matthew 22. 15-22.

XXV

O LORD, we beseech thee, absolve thy people from their offences; that through thy bountiful goodness we may all be delivered from the bands of those sins, which by our frailty we have committed: Grant this, O heavenly Father, for Jesus Christ's sake, our blessed Lord and Saviour. *Amen.*

Colossians 1. 3-13.

St. Matthew 9. 18-26.

XXVI

STIR up, we beseech thee, O Lord, the wills of thy faithful people; that they, plenteously bringing forth the fruit of good works, may of thee be plenteously rewarded; through Jesus Christ our Lord. *Amen.*

Jeremiah 23. 5-8.

St. John 6. 5-14.

ALL SAINTS' DAY
(November 1)

At this time we remember the faithful in Christ who have finished their course on earth; and we pray that, encouraged by their examples and strengthened by their fellowship, we also may be found meet to be partakers of the inheritance of the saints in light.

O ALMIGHTY God, who hast knit together thine elect in one communion and fellowship, in the mystical body of thy Son Christ our Lord: Grant us grace so to follow thy blessed saints in all virtuous and godly living, that we may come to those unspeakable joys, which thou hast prepared for them that unfeignedly love thee; through Jesus Christ our Lord. *Amen.*

Or this.

O GOD, who hast brought us near to an innumerable company of angels, and to the spirits of just men made perfect: Grant us during our earthly pilgrimage to abide in their fellowship, and in our heavenly country to become partakers of their joy; through Jesus Christ our Lord. *Amen.*

Or this.

LORD of all worlds, we bless thy name for all those who have entered into their rest, and reached the promised land, where thou art seen face to face. Give us grace to be followers of them, as they followed in the footsteps of thy holy Son. Encourage our wavering hearts by their example, and help us to see in them the pledges of thy might by which the weak are made strong. Keep alive in us the memory of our beloved whom thou hast called out of this world, and make it powerful to subdue every unworthy thought and wish. Grant that every remembrance that turns our hearts to the unseen may lead them upward to thee, till we also come to the eternal rest which thou hast prepared for thy people, through Jesus Christ. *Amen.*

Revelation 7. 9-17, *or* Hebrews 11. 32 to 12. 2.

St. Matthew 5. 1-12.

THE FESTIVAL OF THE DEDICATION OF A CHURCH

O GOD, by whose providence we celebrate again the consecration (*or* dedication) of this Church: Send down upon us, we beseech thee, thy heavenly blessing; and, because holiness becometh thine house for ever, make us thy living temples, holy and acceptable unto thee; through Jesus Christ our Lord. *Amen.*

1 Corinthians 3. 9-17, *or* 1 St. Peter 2. 1-5.

St. Matthew 21. 12-16, *or* St. John 10. 22-29.

THE MISSIONARY WORK OF THE CHURCH

O GOD, who hast made of one blood all nations of men to dwell on the face of the earth, and didst send thy blessed Son Jesus Christ to preach peace to them that are afar off, and to them that are nigh: Grant that all the peoples of the world may feel after thee and find thee; and hasten, O Lord, the fulfilment of thy promise, to pour out thy Spirit upon all flesh; through Jesus Christ our Lord. *Amen.*

Isaiah 2. 2-4, *or* 42. 1-16, *or* 55.

Romans 1. 1-17, *or* Ephesians 2. 13-22.

St. Matthew 28. 18-20, *or* St. Mark 16. 9-20, *or* St. Luke 10. 1-20, *or* St. John 1. 35-51.

THE NEW YEAR

O ALMIGHTY God, who alone art without variableness or shadow of turning, and hast safely brought us through the changes of time to the beginning of another year: We beseech thee to pardon the sins we have committed in the year which is past, and give us grace that we may spend the remainder of our days to thy honour and glory; through Jesus Christ our Lord. *Amen.*

Or this.

ETERNAL God, who makest all things new, and abidest for ever the same: Grant us to commence this year in thy faith, and to continue it in thy favour; that, being guided in all our doings, and guarded all our days, we may spend our lives in thy service, and finally, by thy grace, attain the glory of everlasting life; through Jesus Christ our Lord. *Amen.*

Revelation 21. 1-7, *or* Philippians 3. 1-14.

St. Matthew 25. 31-46, *or* St. Luke 9. 57-62.

DOMINION DAY

ALMIGHTY God, who didst lead our fathers into this land, and set their feet in a large room: Give thy grace, we beseech thee, to us their children, that we may approve ourselves a people mindful of thy favour, and glad to do thy will. Bless our Dominion with honourable industry, sound learning, and pure manners. Save us from lawlessness and discord, pride and arrogance, and fashion into one godly people the multitude brought hither out of many kindreds and tongues. Give to all the spirit of service, love, and mutual forbearance. In prosperity make us thankful unto thee, and in the day of trouble suffer not our trust in thee to fail. So that, loving thee above all things, we may fulfil thy gracious purpose in this land; through Jesus Christ our Lord. *Amen.*

Deuteronomy 8, *or* 10. 12-22 and 11. 8-12.

St. Matthew 6. 19-33.

A TABLE OF LESSONS

A DAY OF HARVEST THANKSGIVING

ALMIGHTY and everlasting God, who hast graciously given to us the fruits of the earth in their season: We yield thee humble and hearty thanks for these thy bounties, beseeching thee to give us grace rightly to use them to thy glory and the relief of those that need; through Jesus Christ our Lord. *Amen.*

Deuteronomy 26. 1-11.

1 Corinthians 3. 6-15, *or* Galatians 6. 6-10.

St. Luke 12. 13-34, *or* St. John 4. 31-36, *or* 6. 26-40.

AN ORDER FOR THE CELEBRATION OF

THE LORD'S SUPPER

OR

HOLY COMMUNION

THE INTRODUCTION

¶ *The Service shall begin with a Psalm or Hymn shewing forth the power, the goodness, and the grace of God.*

¶ *Then shall the Minister pray in this wise, he and the People humbly seeking the mercy of God.*

ALMIGHTY God, unto whom all hearts be open, all desires known, and from whom no secrets are hid: Cleanse the thoughts of our hearts by the inspiration of thy Holy Spirit, that we may perfectly love thee, and worthily magnify thy holy name; through Christ our Lord. *Amen.*

¶ *Here may follow Confession; or else the Minister shall say,*

O LORD God, hear us when we make our common supplications unto thee.

For the peace that is from above, and for the loving kindness of our God, we make our supplication unto thee.

For the peace of the whole world, for the well-being of the churches of God, and for the unity of them all, we make our supplication unto thee.

For this house of prayer, and for all that with faith, reverence, and the fear of God enter here, we make our supplication unto thee.

Remembering what thy love hath wrought in thy saints, and thy faithfulness to our fathers and brethren who are now with thee, we commend ourselves, and one another, and all our life, to Christ our Lord.

Help, save, pity, and defend us, O God, by thy grace. *Amen.*

¶ *The shall be sung or said this Litany* (*The Hymnary, No.* 758).

Lord, have mercy.
Christ, have mercy.
Lord, have mercy.

¶ *Then shall be sung or said* Gloria in excelsis (*The Hymnary, No.* 750), *or* Benedictus (*The Hymnary, No.* 753); *or else, a Hymn of praise and humble gratitude to God.*

¶ *Instead of the foregoing Introduction, the Minister may, if he will, use the Introduction of either Directory for Public Worship.*

THE MINISTRY OF THE WORD

¶ *Then shall be said a Prayer for Grace* (*pages* 75 *to* 109).

¶ *Then shall be read a Lesson from the Old Testament, or a Lesson from an Epistle, or both* (*pages* 75 *to* 109).

¶ *Here a Psalm or part of a Psalm may be sung or said.*

¶ *Then shall a part of one of the Gospels be read* (*pages* 75 *to* 109).

¶ *Here a Hymn may be sung.*

¶ *Then the Minister shall make such Announcements as are needful and fitting.*

¶ *Then shall follow the Sermon.*

¶ *The Sermon being ended, the Minister may give an Exhortation, using, if he will, that placed at the end of this Order.*

THE HOLY COMMUNION

¶ *Here the Offerings of the People shall be collected and presented; and the Bread and Wine shall be prepared for the Sacrament; and a Psalm or Hymn may be sung.*

¶ *Then shall follow Intercession for the Church, for the Nation, and for All Men, and Commemoration of the Departed.*

¶ *Here may be read the narrative of the institution of the Lord's Supper.* 1 Corinthians 11: 23-26.

¶ *Then shall the Minister say,*

YE that do truly and earnestly repent of your sins, and are in love and charity with your neighbours, and intend to lead a new life, following the commandments of God, and walking from henceforth in his holy ways: Draw near with faith, and take this holy Sacrament to your comfort; and make your humble confession to Almighty God.

Then shall this general Confession be said by the Minister and all the People (*The Hymnary, after No.* 770).

ALMIGHTY God, Father of our Lord Jesus Christ, Maker of all things, Judge of all men: We acknowledge and confess our manifold sins, Which we, from time to time, have committed, By thought, word, and deed, Against thy Divine Majesty. We do earnesly repent, And are heartily sorry for these our misdoings; The remembrance of them is grievous unto us. Have mercy upon us, Have mercy upon us, most merciful Father; For thy Son our Lord Jesus Christ's sake, Forgive us all that is past; And grant that we may ever hereafter Serve and please thee In newness of life, To the honour and glory of thy name; Through Jesus Christ our Lord. Amen.

Here the Minister shall say,

ALMIGHTY God, our heavenly Father, who of thy great mercy hast promised forgiveness of sins to all them that with hearty repentance and true faith turn unto thee: Have mercy upon us; pardon and deliver us from all our sins; confirm and strengthen us in all goodness; and bring us to everlasting life; through Jesus Christ our Lord. *Amen.*

¶ *Here the Minister shall say to the People,*

Hear what comfortable words our Saviour Christ saith unto all that truly turn to him.

COME unto me, all ye that labour and are heavy laden, and I will give you rest. *St. Matthew* 11. 28.

God so loved the world, that he gave his only begotten Son, that whosoever believeth in him should not perish, but have everlasting life. *St. John* 3. 16.

Hear also what Saint Paul saith.

This is a true saying, and worthy of all acceptation, That Jesus Christ came into the world to save sinners. *1 Timothy* 1. 15.

Hear also what Saint John saith.

If any man sin, we have an Advocate with the Father, Jesus Christ the righteous; and he is the propitiation for our sins.
1 St. John 2. 1, 2.

¶ *Then shall the Minister say,*

Let us pray.

WE do not presume to come to this thy Table, O merciful Lord, trusting in our own righteousness, but in thy manifold and great mercies. We are not worthy so much as to gather up the crumbs under thy Table. But thou art the same Lord, whose property is always to have mercy: Grant us therefore, gracious Lord, so to eat the Flesh of thy dear Son Jesus Christ, and to drink his Blood, that our sinful bodies may be made clean by his Body, and our souls washed through his most precious Blood, and that we may evermore dwell in him, and he in us. *Amen.*

¶ *Instead of the foregoing Invitation, Confession, Prayer for Pardon, Comfortable Words, and Prayer of Humble Access, may be said the following Prayer.*

O GOD, who by the Blood of thy dear Son hast consecrated for us a new and living way into the holiest of all: Grant unto us, we beseech thee, the assurance of thy mercy, and sanctify us by thy Holy Spirit, that, drawing near unto thee with a pure heart and undefiled conscience, we may offer unto thee a sacrifice in righteousness; through Jesus Christ our Lord. *Amen.*

¶ *Then shall the Minister say, and the People answer, as followeth.*

Minister. The Lord be with you;

People. And with thy spirit.

Minister. Lift up your hearts;

People. We lift them up unto the Lord.

Minister. Let us give thanks unto our Lord God;

People. It is meet and right so to do.

Then the Minister, proceeding, shall say,

IT is very meet, right, and our bounden duty, that we should at all times, and in all places, give thanks unto thee, O Holy Lord, Father Almighty, Everlasting God, who didst create the heavens and the earth and all that in them is, who didst make man in thine own image, and whose tender mercies are over all thy works.

Here may follow one of the Prefaces placed at the end of this Order, or else immediately shall follow,

THEREFORE with angels and archangels and with all the company of heaven, we laud and magnify thy glorious name; evermore praising thee, and saying,

HOLY, holy, holy, Lord God of hosts,
Heaven and earth are full of thy glory.
Glory be to thee, O Lord most high.

And the Minister shall continue thus,

ALL glory and thanksgiving be to thee, Almighty God, our heavenly Father, for that thou of thy tender mercy didst give thine only Son Jesus Christ to take our nature upon him, and to suffer death upon the Cross for our redemption; who made there a full, perfect, and sufficient sacrifice for the sins of the whole world; and did institute, and in his holy Gospel, command us to continue, a perpetual memory of that his precious death until his coming again;

Who, the same night in which he was betrayed, took bread, and when he had given thanks, he brake it, and said, Take, eat, this is my Body, which is broken for you; this do in remembrance of me. After the same manner also he took the cup, saying, This cup is the new Covenant in my Blood; this do ye, as oft as ye drink it, in remembrance of me.

Wherefore, having in remembrance his precious death and passion, his glorious resurrection and ascension, and pleading his eternal sacrifice, we thy servants do set forth this memorial which he hath willed us to make, giving thee thanks that thou hast counted us worthy to stand before thee.

And we most humbly beseech thee, O merciful Father, to vouchsafe unto us thy gracious presence, and so to sanctify with thy Word and Spirit these thine own gifts of bread and wine which we set before thee, that the bread which we break may be to us the Communion of the Body of Christ, and the cup of blessing which we bless the Communion of the Blood of Christ.

And we entirely desire thy fatherly goodness mercifully to accept this our sacrifice of praise and thanksgiving; most humbly beseeching thee to grant, that by the merits and death of thy Son Jesus Christ, we and thy whole Church may obtain remission of our sins, and all other benefits of his passion.

And here we offer and present unto thee, O Lord, ourselves, our souls and bodies, to be a reasonable, holy, and living sacrifice unto thee: humbly beseeching thee, that all we, who are partakers of this Holy Communion, may be fulfilled with thy grace and heavenly benediction.

And although we be unworthy, through our manifold sins, to offer unto thee any sacrifice, yet we beseech thee to accept this our bounden duty and service, not weighing our merits, but pardoning our offences;

Through Jesus Christ our Lord, by whom and with whom in the unity of the Holy Spirit, all honour and glory be unto thee, O Father Almighty, world without end. *Amen.*

And now, as our Saviour Christ hath taught us, we say,

OUR Father, who art in heaven, Hallowed be thy name; Thy kingdom come; Thy will be done; In earth as it is in heaven. Give us this day our daily bread. And forgive us our trespasses, As we forgive them that trespass against us. And lead us not into temptation; But deliver us from evil; For thine is the kingdom, The power, and the glory, For ever and ever. Amen.

¶ *Then the Minister shall say,*

ACCORDING to the holy example of our Lord Jesus Christ, and in remembrance of him, we do this; who, the same night in which he was betrayed, took bread;

Here he shall take the Bread in his hands.

And when he had given thanks, as we do now give thanks to thee, O eternal Father, he brake it,

Here he shall break the Bread.

And said, Take, eat, this is my Body which is broken for you; this do in remembrance of me.

After the same manner also he took the Cup;

Here he shall take the Cup into his hands.

Saying, This Cup is the New Covenant in my Blood; this do ye, as oft as ye drink it, in remembrance of me.

¶ *Then shall the Minister say,*

THE peace of the Lord Jesus Christ be with you all.

¶ *Then shall the Minister and the People receive the Communion. And when the Minister delivereth the Bread, he shall say,*

THE Body of our Lord Jesus Christ, which was given for *thee*, preserve *thee* unto everlasting life. Take and eat this in remembrance that Christ died for *thee*, and feed on him in *thy* heart by faith with thanksgiving.

Or,

Take, eat; this is the Body of Christ which is broken for you; do this in remembrance of him.

And when the Minister delivereth the Cup, he shall say,

THE Blood of our Lord Jesus Christ, which was shed for *thee*, preserve *thee* unto everlasting life. Drink this in remembrance that Christ's Blood was shed for *thee*, and be thankful.

Or,

THIS Cup is the New Covenant in the Blood of Christ, which is shed for the remission of the sins of many; drink ye all of it.

¶ *When all have communicated, what remaineth of the sacred Elements shall be reverently placed upon the Table, and covered with a fair linen cloth.*

¶ *Then shall the Minister give thanks to God, and beseech his grace, in the name of all them that have communicated, saying,*

HEAVENLY Father, we give thee praise and thanks that upon us the unworthy thou dost confer so rich a benefit as to bring us into the communion of thy Son Jesus Christ; whom, having delivered up to death, thou hast given for our nourishment unto eternal life. Now also grant us grace, that we may never be unmindful of these things; but bearing them about, engraven on our hearts, may advance and grow in that faith which is effectual unto every good work; through Jesus Christ our Lord. *Amen.*

Here one or more Post-Communion Prayers may be said.

And this Prayer may be added.

WE remember before thee the multitude of every name who are joined with us throughout the world. O Lord, save thy people and bless thine inheritance; feed them also, and lift them up for ever. And we bless thy holy name for all thy servants who have finished their course, especially those dear to our own souls who have entered into thy rest. And rejoicing that we are still one with them in the same holy fellowship, we pray that we may be united with them in the joy and peace of the perfect life; through Jesus Christ our Lord. *Amen.*

¶ *Then may a Hymn be sung.*

¶ *Then shall the Minister let the People depart with this Blessing.*

THE peace of God, which passeth all understanding, keep your hearts and minds in the knowledge and love of God, and of his Son Jesus Christ our Lord; and the blessing of God Almighty, the Father, the Son, and the Holy Spirit, be amongst you and remain with you always. *Amen.*

Or else this.

NOW the God of peace, that brought again from the dead our Lord Jesus, that great Shepherd of the sheep, through the blood of the everlasting covenant, make you perfect in every good work to do his will, working in you that which is well-pleasing in his sight, through Jesus Christ; to whom be glory for ever and ever. *Amen.*

¶ *If desired, a Creed may be said or sung either after the Gospel or after the Sermon; or the Hymn* Te Deum (*The Hymnary, No.* 748) *may be sung.*

¶ *It is to be noted that for the Prayers beginning* All glory and thanksgiving *and ending with the Lord's Prayer, may be substituted the corresponding Prayer of the second Order.*

¶ *It is to be noted that the Intercession may be joined with the Prayers of Consecration and be followed by the Lord's Prayer.*

¶ *Where it is customary, a second Offering, for benevolent purposes, may be taken before the last Hymn is sung.*

APPENDIX

The following are for use with both Orders of Holy Communion.

THE NICENE CREED

I BELIEVE in one God, the Father Almighty, Maker of heaven and earth, And of all things visible and invisible:

And in one Lord Jesus Christ, the only-begotten Son of God, Begotten of his Father before all worlds, God of God, Light of Light, Very God of very God, Begotten, not made, Being of one substance with the Father, By whom all things were made: Who for us men, and for our salvation came down from heaven, And was incarnate by the Holy Ghost of the Virgin Mary, And was made man, and was crucified also for us under Pontius Pilate. He suffered and was buried, And the third day he rose again according to the Scriptures, And ascended into heaven, And sitteth on the right hand of the Father. And he shall come again with glory to judge both the quick and the dead: Whose kingdom shall have no end.

And I believe in the Holy Ghost, The Lord the giver of life, Who proceedeth from the Father and the Son, Who with the Father and the Son together is worshipped and glorified, Who spake by the Prophets.

And I believe in One Holy Catholic and

Apostolic Church. I acknowledge one Baptism for the remission of sins. And I look for the Resurrection of the dead, And the Life of the world to come. Amen.

AN EXHORTATION

Which may be used at the close of the Sermon.

DEARLY beloved, as we draw near to the Lord's Table to celebrate the Holy Communion of the Body and Blood of Christ, we are gratefully to remember that this Sacrament was instituted as a memorial of his undying love for us, as a seal of our bond of union with him and with each other as members of his mystical Body, and as a pledge of his faithfulness unto them that are called to the marriage-supper of the Lamb.

Let us consider earnestly our great need of having our comfort and strength so renewed in this our earthly pilgrimage and warfare; and especially how necessary it is that we come to the Lord's Table with knowledge and love, and with hearts hungering and thirsting after Christ. Not unto those who live willingly in transgression and offences, nor unto those who cherish pride and self-righteousness in their hearts, are these benefits of Christ offered. But all that are truly sorry for their sins, and would be delivered from the burden of them, all that humbly put their trust in

Christ, and desire his grace that they may live a holy life, are encouraged and invited in his name to come to this Sacrament. Let us so come that we may find refreshing and rest unto our souls.

INTERCESSIONS

Either the first or the second of the Intercessions following may be used after the Offerings are presented; or the third may be used immediately before the Lord's Prayer.

I

O GOD, our heavenly Father, we beseech thee to receive the humble intercessions, which, through the merits and mediation of thy Son, we offer unto thee.

Remember, O Lord, thy holy Church upon earth; increase and sanctify it more and more; reveal thy glory among all nations; and hasten the victory of thine eternal kingdom.

Remember, O Lord, our Country and Empire, our King and all who rule over us; grant unto them grace and guidance, and bless our land with righteousness and peace.

Remember, O Lord, all who are in sickness, sorrow, and bereavement, and those to whom death draws near. . . . Visit them with thy love and consolation, and grant them thy peace; through Jesus Christ our Lord.

And rejoicing in the communion of saints,

we remember with thanksgiving all thy redeemed, and those dear to ourselves, who are asleep in Jesus. . . . And we beseech thee to give us grace to be followers of them as they were followers of Christ, that we with them may attain eternal rest and peace; through Jesus Christ our Lord, to whom, with thee and the Holy Spirit, be all honour and glory, world without end. *Amen.*

II

ALMIGHTY and everliving God, who by thy holy Apostle hast taught us to make prayers, and supplications, and to give thanks, for all men: We humbly beseech thee most mercifully receive these our prayers, which we offer unto thy Divine Majesty; beseeching thee to inspire continually the universal Church with the spirit of truth, unity, and concord. And grant, that all they that do confess thy holy name may agree in the truth of thy holy Word, and live in unity, and godly love.

We beseech thee also to lead all Christian Kings, Princes, and Governors; and especially thy servant George our King, that under him thy people may be godly and quietly governed. And grant unto all that are put in authority under him, that they may honestly and impartially administer justice, to the punishment of wickedness and vice, and to the maintenance of thy true religion, and virtue.

Give grace, O heavenly Father, to all Ministers of thy Church, that they may both by their life and doctrine set forth thy true and living Word and rightly and duly administer thy holy Sacraments.

And to all thy people give thy heavenly grace; and especially to this congregation here present; that, with meek heart and due reverence, they may hear, and receive thy holy Word; truly serving thee in holiness and righteousness all the days of their life.

And we most humbly beseech thee of thy goodness, O Lord, to comfort and succour all them, who in this transitory life are in trouble, sorrow, need, sickness, or any other adversity.

And we also bless thy holy name for all thy servants departed this life in thy faith and fear; beseeching thee to give us grace so to follow their good examples, that with them we may be partakers of thy heavenly kingdom.

Grant this, O Father, for Jesus Christ's sake, our only Mediator and Advocate. *Amen.*

III

O MOST merciful God, behold this our offering, and have regard to the Sacrifice offered once for all upon the Cross, and accept our humble prayers.

We remember thy holy Church throughout all the world, beseeching thee to vouchsafe unto us and to all thy people the fullness of thy redeeming grace; through Jesus Christ our Lord.

We remember those of thy flock who are in sickness, poverty, sorrow, and temptation, and those to whom death draws near, . . . , beseeching thee to grant unto them life and salvation; through Jesus Christ our Lord.

And we remember with thanksgiving the faithful and blessed departed, and our beloved ones whom thou hast taken to thyself . . . , beseeching thee to bring us with them to those things which eye hath not seen, nor ear heard, which thou hast prepared for them that love thee; through Jesus Christ our Lord, to whom, with thee and the Holy Spirit, be all honour and glory, world without end. *Amen.*

Matter of Intercession may also be found on pages 35 to 56.

THE NARRATIVE OF THE INSTITUTION OF THE LORD'S SUPPER ACCORDING TO ST. PAUL

I HAVE received of the Lord that which also I delivered unto you, That the Lord Jesus the same night in which he was betrayed took bread: And when he had given thanks, he brake it, and said, Take, eat: this is my body, which is broken for you: this do in remembrance of me. After the same manner also he took the cup, when he had supped, saying, This cup is the new testament in my blood: this do ye, as oft as ye drink it, in remembrance of me. For as often as ye eat this bread, and drink this cup, ye do shew the Lord's death till he come.

1 *Corinthians* 11. 23-26.

PREFACES PROPER TO PARTICULAR TIMES

These Prefaces may be said after the words Whose tender mercies are over all thy works (*page* 115).

At Christmas

AND who didst give Jesus Christ thine only Son to be born for us, that by taking flesh of our humanity he might make us partakers of the divine glory. Therefore with angels, etc.

At Easter

BUT chiefly are we bound to praise thee for the glorious resurrection of thy Son Jesus Christ our Lord; For he is the very Paschal Lamb, which was offered for us, and hath taken away the sin of the world; Who by his death hath destroyed death, and by his rising to life hath begotten us again unto a living hope. Therefore with angels, etc.

At Pentecost

AND who didst pour forth upon the Church thy Holy and Life-giving Spirit: That through his power the everlasting gospel might go forth into all the world: Whereby we have been brought out of darkness and error into the clear light and true knowledge of thee and of thy Son our Saviour Jesus Christ. Therefore with angels, etc.

On All Saints' Day

Or at any time when the Righteous Dead are remembered.

AND who, in the righteousness of thy saints, hast given us an example of godly living, and in their blessedness the hope of our calling: That, being compassed about with so great a cloud of witnesses, we may run with patience the race that is set before us, and with them receive the crown of glory that fadeth not away. Therefore with angels, etc.

At the Dedication of a Church or the Anniversary Thereof

AND who, though the heaven of heavens cannot contain thee and thy glory is in all the world: Dost deign to hallow places for thy worship, and in them dost pour forth gifts of grace upon thy faithful people. Therefore with angels, etc.

AN ANTHEM

(*The Hymnary, No.* 756).

Which may be sung immediately after the words Glory be to thee, O Lord most high; *or immediately before the Lord's Prayer.*

BLESSED is he that cometh in the name of the Lord: Hosanna in the highest.

AN ANTHEM

(*The Hymnary, No.* 757.)

Which may be sung at the time when Minister and People receive the Communion.

O LAMB of God, that takest away the sins of the world: Have mercy upon us.
O Lamb of God, that takest away the sins of the world: Have mercy upon us.
O Lamb of God, that takest away the sins of the world: Grant us thy peace.

POST-COMMUNION PRAYERS

Which may be used after the Prayer beginning, Heavenly Father, we give thee praise; *but the last of them may be used instead of that Prayer.*

For Complete Consecration.

GRANT, O Lord, that the ears which have heard the voice of thy songs may be closed to the voice of clamour and dispute; that the eyes which have seen thy great love may also behold thy blessed hope; that the tongues which have sung thy praise may speak the truth; that the feet which have walked thy courts may walk in the region of light; and that the bodies which have tasted thy living Body may be restored in newness of life. Glory be to thee for thine unspeakable gift. *Amen.*

For Answer to all our Needs.

ALMIGHTY God, the fountain of all wisdom, who knowest our necessities before we ask, and our ignorance in asking: We beseech thee to have compassion upon our infirmities; and those things which for our unworthiness we dare not, and for our blindness we cannot ask, vouchsafe to give us, for the worthiness of thy Son Jesus Christ our Lord. *Amen.*

Thanksgiving for Communion and Prayer for grace to persevere.

ALMIGHTY and everliving God, we most heartily thank thee that in thy great love thou dost vouchsafe to feed us at thy Table with this spiritual food, and dost assure us thereby of thy favour towards us, and that we are very members incorporate in the mystical Body of thy Son, and heirs through hope of thy everlasting kingdom. And we most humbly beseech thee, O heavenly Father, so to assist us with thy grace that we may continue in that holy fellowship, and do all such works as thou hast prepared for us to walk in; through Jesus Christ our Lord. *Amen.*

Many other Prayers for Grace in this book are suitable for use here.

ANOTHER ORDER FOR THE CELEBRATION OF

THE LORD'S SUPPER

OR

HOLY COMMUNION

¶ *The Service shall proceed after the usual Order for Public Worship as far as the Sermon, the Minister remembering always that the Prayers set down in the Order following are the main Prayers of the Service. At the end of the Sermon the Minister may give an Exhortation, using, if he will, that placed at the end of the foregoing Order.*

¶ *Then the Offerings of the People shall be collected and presented, if this has not been done already; and the Bread and the Wine shall be prepared for the Sacrament; and a Psalm or Hymn may be sung.*

¶ *Then shall follow Intercession for the Church, for the Nation, and for all Men, and Commemoration of the Departed.*

¶ *Here may be read the narrative of the institution of the Lord's Supper.* 1 Corinthians 11: 23-26.

¶ *Then shall the Minister say,*

Let us make our humble confession to Almighty God.

And this general Confession shall be said by the Minister and all the People (*The Hymnary, after No.* 770).

ALMIGHTY God, Father of our Lord Jesus Christ, Maker of all things, Judge of all men: We acknowledge and confess our manifold sins, Which we from time to time have committed, By thought, word, and deed, Against thy Divine Majesty. We do earnestly repent, And are heartily sorry for these our misdoings; The remembrance of them is grievous unto us. Have mercy upon us, most merciful Father. For thy Son our Lord Jesus Christ's sake, Forgive us all that is past; And grant that we may ever hereafter Serve and please thee In newness of life, To the honour and glory of thy name; Through Jesus Christ our Lord. Amen.

And the Minister shall continue as followeth.

ALMIGHTY God, our heavenly Father, who of thy great mercy hast promised forgiveness of sins to all them that with hearty repentance and true faith turn unto thee: Have mercy upon us; pardon and deliver us from all our sins; confirm and strengthen us in all goodness; and bring us to everlasting life; through Jesus Christ our Lord. *Amen.*

Or else, instead of the two foregoing paragraphs this Confession following shall be said by Minister and People, with the Sentence (of the Minister) following.

WE confess to God, Father, Son, and Holy Spirit, and to all the company of heaven, and to one another, that we have sinned, in thought, word, and deed, and by omission, through our fault, our own fault, our own grievous fault; wherefore we pray

Almighty God to have mercy upon us, to forgive us our sins, and to make clean our hearts within us.

And the Minister shall continue as followeth.

MAY the almighty and merciful Lord grant us pardon, absolution, and remission of our sins. *Amen.*

¶ *Then shall the Minister say,*

THE peace of the Lord Jesus Christ be with you all.

¶ *Then shall the Minister say,*

AS our Lord Jesus Christ, the night in which he was betrayed, took bread, so I take these elements of bread and wine to be set apart to this holy use.

Here the Minister shall lay his hand upon the Plate and the Cup.

And as he gave thanks and blessed, let us lift up our hearts, and give thanks to our Lord God.

IT is very meet, right, and our bounden duty, that we should at all times and in all places, give thanks unto thee, O Holy Lord, Father Almighty, Everlasting God, who didst create the heavens and the earth and all that in them is, who didst make man in thine own image, and whose tender mercies are over all thy works. Therefore with angels and archangels and with all the company of heaven, we laud and magnify thy glorious name; evermore praising thee, and saying,

HOLY, holy, holy, Lord God of hosts,
Heaven and earth are full of thy glory.
Glory be to thee, O Lord most high.

And the Minister shall continue thus.

ALL glory and thanksgiving be to thee, Almighty God, our heavenly Father, for that thou of thy tender mercy didst give thine only Son Jesus Christ to take our nature upon him, and to suffer death upon the Cross for our redemption; who made there a full, perfect, and sufficient sacrifice for the sins of the whole world; and did institute, and in his holy Gospel command us to continue, a perpetual memory of that his precious death until his coming again;

Who, the same night in which he was betrayed, took bread, and when he had given thanks, he brake it, and said, Take, eat, this is my Body, which is broken for you; this do in remembrance of me. After the same manner also he took the cup, saying, This cup is the new Covenant in my Blood; this do ye, as oft as ye drink it, in remembrance of me.

Not as we ought, but as we are able, do we bless thee for his holy incarnation, for his perfect life on earth, for his precious sufferings and death upon the Cross, for his glorious resurrection and ascension, and for the promise of his coming again.

And we most humbly beseech thee, O merciful Father, to look upon us as we do now make that memorial of his blessed sacrifice which he hath commanded us to make; and send down thy Holy Spirit to bless and consecrate these thine own gifts of bread and wine which we set before thee, that the bread which we break may be unto us the Communion of the Body of Christ, and the cup of blessing which we bless the Communion of the Blood of Christ; that we, receiving them, may by faith be made partakers of his Body and Blood, to our spiritual nourishment and growth in grace, and to the glory of thy holy name. *Amen.*

OUR Father, who art in heaven, Hallowed be thy name; Thy kingdom come; Thy will be done; In earth as it is in heaven. Give us this day our daily bread. And forgive us our trespasses, As we forgive them that trespass against us. And lead us not into temptation; But deliver us from evil; For thine is the kingdom, The power, and the glory, For ever and ever. Amen.

¶ *Then shall the Minister say,*

ACCORDING to the holy example of our Lord Jesus Christ, and in remembrance of him, we do this; who, the same night in which he was betrayed took bread;

Here he shall take the Bread into his hands.

And when he had given thanks, as we do now give thanks to thee, O eternal Father, he brake it,

Here he shall break the Bread.

And said, Take, eat, this is my Body which is broken for you; this do in remembrance of me.

After the same manner also he took the Cup;

Here he shall take the Cup into his hands.

Saying, This Cup is the New Covenant in my Blood; this do ye, as oft as ye drink it, in remembrance of me.

¶ *Then shall the Minister and the People receive the Communion.*

And when the Minister delivereth the Bread, he shall say,

THE Body of our Lord Jesus Christ, which was given for *thee*, preserve *thee* unto everlasting life. Take and eat this in remembrance that Christ died for *thee*, and feed on him in *thy* heart by faith with thanksgiving.

Or else,

TAKE, eat; this is the Body of Christ which is broken for you; do this in remembrance of him.

And when the Minister delivereth the Cup, he shall say,

THE Blood of our Lord Jesus Christ, which was shed for *thee,* preserve *thee* unto everlasting life. Drink this in remembrance that Christ's Blood was shed for *thee,* and be thankful.

Or else.

THIS Cup is the New Covenant in the Blood of Christ, which is shed for the remission of the sins of many; drink ye all of it.

¶ *When all have communicated, what remaineth of the sacred Elements shall be reverently placed upon the Table, and covered with a fair linen cloth.*

¶ *Then shall the Minister give thanks to God, and beseech his grace, in the name of all them that have communicated, saying,*

HEAVENLY Father, we give thee praise and thanks that upon us the unworthy thou dost confer so rich a benefit as to bring us into the communion of thy Son Jesus Christ; whom, having delivered up to death, thou hast given for our nourishment unto eternal life. Now also grant us grace, that we may never be unmindful of these things; but bearing them about, engraven on our hearts, may advance and grow in that faith which is effectual unto every good work; through Jesus Christ our Lord. *Amen.*

Here one or more Post-Communion Prayers may be said.

¶ *Then may a Hymn be sung.*

¶ *Then shall the Minister let the People depart with this Blessing.*

THE peace of God, which passeth all understanding, keep your hearts and minds in the knowledge and love of God, and of his Son Jesus Christ our Lord: and the blessing of God Almighty, the Father, the Son, and the Holy Spirit, be amongst you and remain with you always. *Amen.*

Or this.

NOW the God of peace, that brought again from the dead our Lord Jesus, that great Shepherd of the sheep, through the blood of the everlasting covenant, make you perfect in every good work to do his will, working in you that which is well-pleasing in his sight, through Jesus Christ; to whom be glory for ever and ever. *Amen.*

¶ *If desired, a Creed may be said or sung either after the Gospel or after the Sermon; or the Hymn* Te Deum (*The Hymnary, No.* 748) *may be sung.*

¶ *It is to be noted that for the Prayers beginning* All Glory and thanksgiving *and ending with the Lord's Prayer, may be substituted the corresponding Prayers of the first Order.*

¶ *It is to be noted that the Intercession may be joined with the Prayers of Consecration and be followed by the Lord's Prayer.*

¶ *Where it is customary, a second Offering, for benevolent purposes, may be taken before the last Hymn is sung.*

¶ *If it should happen that a shorter Service is needed, the Order for the Communion of the Sick may be used* (*pages* 178 *to* 182).

AN ORDER FOR

THE BAPTISM OF CHILDREN

¶ *The Minister may, before the administration of the Sacrament, give instruction touching its nature and meaning, using, if he will, the Exhortation placed at the end of this Order.*

THE INTRODUCTION

¶ *The Minister, standing at the Font, shall say to the Parents (or Sponsors) of the child,*

DO you here present this child, earnestly desiring that *he* be received by Holy Baptism into the fellowship of the Church of Christ?

Answer. I do.

¶ *Then shall the Minister say one or other of the Prayers following.*

ALMIGHTY God and merciful Father, who of thine infinite goodness hast called us into thy Church, and promised to be our God and the God and Father of our children: Graciously look upon this child, whom we now offer and dedicate unto thee; and vouchsafe to receive *him* into the fellowship of thy Son Jesus Christ, that as a living member of his Body *he* may be sanctified by thy Spirit, and made partaker of the fullness of thy heavenly grace; through Jesus Christ our Lord. *Amen.*

ALMIGHTY and immortal God, the aid of all that need, the helper of all that flee to thee for succour, the life of them that believe, and the resurrection of the dead: We call upon thee for this child, whom we bring to thee in this holy Sacrament. Receive *him*, O Lord, as thou hast promised by thy well-beloved Son, saying, Ask, and ye shall have; seek, and ye shall find; knock, and it shall be opened unto you; So give now unto us that ask; let us that seek find; open the gate unto us that knock; that this child may become and ever remain Christ's true disciple, and may attain to the eternal kingdom which thou hast promised by Christ our Lord. *Amen.*

¶ *Then shall the Minister say,*

Hear the words of the Gospel according to Saint Mark, in the tenth chapter, at the thirteenth verse.

THEY brought young children to Christ, that he should touch them; and his disciples rebuked those that brought them. But when Jesus saw it, he was much displeased, and said unto them, Suffer the little children to come unto me, and forbid them not; for of such is the kingdom of God. Verily I say unto you, Whosoever shall not receive the kingdom of God as a little child, he shall not enter therein. And he took them up in his arms, put his hands upon them, and blessed them.

¶ *Then may the Minister make this brief Exhortation upon the words of the Gospel.*

BELOVED, you hear in this Gospel the words of our Saviour Christ, that he commanded the children to be brought unto him; how he blamed those that would have kept them from him; how he exhorteth all men to follow their innocency. You perceive how by outward gesture and deed he declared his good will toward them; for he took them in his arms, he laid his hands upon them, and blessed them. He is the same yesterday and to-day and for ever. Doubt not therefore, but earnestly believe, that he loveth this child; that he is ready to receive *him,* to embrace *him* with the arms of his mercy, and give *him* the blessing of eternal life.

THE PROMISES

¶ *Then shall the Minister say unto the Parents* (*or Sponsors*),

FORASMUCH as you desire and claim these blessings for your child, you will now engage, on your part, to perform those things which God requireth of you, that the good will and pleasure of your heavenly Father may not be hidden from your child.

I ask therefore,

DO you confess Jesus Christ as Saviour and Lord?

Answer. I do so confess.

Do you promise, as God shall give you grace, to bring up this child in the knowledge and love of God, to the end that in all things *he* may grow up into union with Christ?
Answer. I do so promise.

¶ *Then shall follow this Prayer.*

GRANT, O Lord, to these thy servants grace to perform the things which they have promised before thee; and sanctify with thy Spirit this child now to be baptized according to thy Word; through Jesus Christ our Lord. *Amen.*

THE BAPTISM

¶ *Then the Minister (taking the child in his arms, or leaving it in the arms of one of the Parents or Sponsors) shall say,*

What is the name of this child?

And then, naming it after them, he shall pour or sprinkle water upon the head of the child, or dip the child in the water, saying,

N. I BAPTIZE thee In the name of the Father, and of the Son, and of the Holy Ghost. Amen.

Then the Minister shall say,

WE receive this child into the congregation of Christ's flock, that as a member of the family and household of God *he* may be nurtured and grow strong, and continue Christ's faithful servant unto *his* life's end. *Amen.*

And the Minister may bless the child, saying,

THE Lord bless thee, and keep thee: the Lord make his face to shine upon thee, and be gracious unto thee: the Lord lift up his countenance upon thee, and give thee peace. *Amen.*

THE PRAYERS

¶ *Then shall the Minister say,*

Let us pray.

MOST holy and merciful Father, we give thee hearty thanks that thou hast numbered us amongst thy people, and dost also call our children unto thee, marking them with this Sacrament as a singular token and badge of thy love. Wherefore we beseech thee to confirm thy favour more and more toward us, and to take into thy tuition and defence this child, whom we offer and present unto thee with common supplications. Grant that *he* may know thee *his* merciful Father, through thy Holy Spirit working in *his* heart, that *he* may not be ashamed to confess the faith of Christ crucified; but may continue his faithful servant, and so prevail against evil that in the end *he* may obtain the victory, and be exalted into the liberty of thy kingdom; through Jesus Christ our Lord. *Amen.*

Or else,

MOST holy and merciful Father, who dost not only beautify and bless us with common benefits, but dost also heap upon us most abundantly rare and wonderful gifts: We lift up our eyes and minds unto thee, and give thee most humble thanks, who dost call our children unto thee, marking them with this Sacrament as a singular token and badge of thy love. Confirm this thy favour more and more towards us, we beseech thee, and take this infant into thy tuition and defence, that *he* may perceive thee continually to be *his* merciful Father, through thy Spirit working in *his* heart, by whose divine power *he* may so prevail against evil, that in the end, obtaining the victory, *he* may be exalted into the liberty of thy kingdom; through Jesus Christ our Lord. *Amen.*

¶ *Then may follow this Prayer for the Home.*

ALMIGHTY God, our heavenly Father, whose blessed Son did share at Nazareth the life of an earthly home: Bless, we beseech thee, the home of this child, and grant wisdom and understanding to all who have the care of *him;* that *he* may grow up in thy constant fear and love; through the same thy Son Jesus Christ our Lord. *Amen.*

Then shall be said by all,

OUR Father, who art in heaven, Hallowed be thy name; Thy kingdom come; Thy will be done; In earth as it is in heaven. Give us this day our daily bread. And forgive us our trespasses, As we forgive them that trespass against us. And lead us not into temptation; But deliver us from evil: For thine is the kingdom, The power, and the glory, For ever and ever. Amen.

THE DUTIES OF THE PEOPLE

¶ *And the Minister shall say to the People this, or the like, Exhortation.*

BRETHREN, this child has now been received into the bosom of the Church of God. You who have participated in this holy act are called, together with the parents (*or* sponsors), to take care that *he* may grow up in the nurture and admonition of the Lord, to lead a godly and Christian life. Consider this your part and duty, and support this child with constant love, and wholesome example, and faithful prayer. May the Lord grant you grace for this work. *Amen.*

¶ *Then the Minister shall say to the Parents* (*or Sponsors*),

Go in the peace of the Lord. *Amen.*

¶ *If the Baptism be administered otherwise than at Public Worship, the Minister shall dismiss them that are gathered with this Blessing.*

THE grace of the Lord Jesus Christ, and the love of God, and the communion of the Holy Spirit, be with you. *Amen.*

¶ *It belongs to the Church, as well as to the Parents* (*or Sponsors*) *to see that children who have been baptized are taught the substance of Christian faith and duty. And when they come to years of discretion they are to own for themselves the covenant of their baptism; they are to confess Jesus Christ as their Saviour and Lord, and engage themselves to be his disciples.*

¶ *In case of extreme urgency it shall suffice if the child be named, and water poured or sprinkled upon its head, with the words,* N., I baptize thee in the name of the Father, and of the Son, and of the Holy Ghost. Amen.

APPENDIX

AN EXHORTATION

Which may be used before the Sacrament of Baptism is administered.

DEARLY beloved, the Father in heaven, who has received us into the fellowship of his Church, has promised to be our God and the God and Father of our children; which covenant he renews in this Sacrament of Baptism given to us as a sign and seal of the washing away of our sins, and our ingrafting into Christ.

You that are fathers and mothers may take hence most singular comfort in seeing your children thus received into the bosom of Christ's Church, and by this you are admonished that you bring them up in piety and virtue, remembering that their Father in heaven careth for them.

A CONFESSION OF FAITH

Which may be used in place of the first question (as equivalent thereto), asked of Parents or Sponsors.

DO you believe in God the Father Almighty, Maker of heaven and earth; and in Jesus Christ, his only Son our Lord, who was born into the world, and who suffered for us; and in the Holy Ghost, the Holy Catholic Church, the Communion of Saints, the Forgiveness of sins, and the Life everlasting?

Answer. I do.

PRAYERS

One or other of which may be used in place of that beginning, Grant, O Lord.

I

ALMIGHTY, everlasting God, whose most dearly beloved Son Jesus Christ, for the forgiveness of our sins, did shed out of his most precious side both water and blood; and gave commandment to his disciples, that they should go teach all nations, and baptize them In the name of the Father, and of the Son, and of the Holy Ghost: Regard, we beseech thee, our supplications; and grant that this child, now to be baptized, may receive the fullness of thy grace, and be found at last in the number of thy faithful and elect children; through Jesus Christ our Lord. *Amen.*

II

ALMIGHTY, everlasting God, whose beloved Son became man for us men and for our salvation, and gave commandment to his disciples, that they should go teach all nations, and baptize them In the name of the

Father, and of the Son, and of the Holy Ghost: Hear, we beseech thee, the prayer of thy people; set apart this water to the holy use unto which thou hast appointed it; and grant that this child, now to be baptized therein, may receive the fullness of thy grace, and ever remain in the number of thy faithful and elect children; through Jesus Christ our Lord. *Amen.*

AN ORDER FOR
THE RECEPTION TO FULL COMMUNION

AND THE CONFIRMATION OF THOSE WHO HAVE BEEN BAPTIZED

¶ *When children who have been baptized are come to years of discretion, and have been taught the substance of Christian faith and duty, they are to be brought before the Church, that they may openly confess for themselves Jesus Christ as their Saviour and Lord. And they are to be assured that their Lord who now comes to them with his grace and strength will never fail them; and in particular that he will meet them at his own Table to their lives' end.*

¶ *Upon the day appointed an Address, touching the meaning of the action, may be given by the Minister. Then all that are to be received shall stand before the Minister, and he shall speak to them in this wise.*

BELOVED in the Lord, in your baptism you were received into the fellowship of Christ, sealed as members of the family and household of God, and engaged to be the Lord's. Now you come, of your own choice, to ratify the solemn covenant and vow then made in your behalf, to profess your faith in the Lord Jesus, and to consecrate yourselves to him. Doubt ye not, but earnestly believe that he waiteth to receive you, and that he will confirm and strengthen you anew by his Holy Spirit, that ye may grow more and more in the knowledge of God, and be enabled to keep his covenant steadfastly to the end.

I ask you therefore before God and this congregation,

DO you believe in God the Father Almighty, Maker of heaven and earth; and in Jesus Christ, his only Son our Lord, who was born into the world, and who suffered for us; and in the Holy Ghost, the Holy Catholic Church, the Communion of Saints, the Forgiveness of sins, and the Life everlasting?

Answer. I do.

WILL you then endeavour to keep God's holy will and commandments, and to walk in the same all the days of your life?

Answer. I will.

DO you promise to make diligent use of the means of grace, and in all things to seek earnestly the peace and welfare of the Church of God?

Answer. I do so promise, God being my helper.

¶ *Then shall the Minister say,*

Let us pray.

ALMIGHTY and everliving God, strengthen, we beseech thee, these thy servants with the Holy Spirit the Comforter, and daily increase in them thy manifold gifts of grace; the spirit of wisdom and understanding; the spirit of counsel and might; the spirit of knowledge and true godliness; fill them, O

God, with the spirit of thy holy fear; and keep them in thy mercy unto life eternal; through Jesus Christ our Lord. *Amen.*

¶ *Then the Minister (laying his hand, if such be his discretion, upon the head of every one in order kneeling before him) shall say,*

THE God of all grace, who hath called you unto his eternal glory by Jesus Christ, confirm you to the end, that ye may be blameless in the day of our Lord Jesus Christ. *Amen.*

Or else,

DEFEND, O Lord, this thy child (*or* servant) with thy heavenly grace, that *he* may continue thine for ever; and daily increase in thy Holy Spirit more and more, until *he* come unto thy everlasting kingdom. *Amen.*

¶ *Then shall the Minister say,*

Let us pray.

ALMIGHTY God, our heavenly Father, we give thee hearty thanks and praise that thou hast not withheld thy loving kindness from these thy children (*or* servants), but hast given them shelter within the covenant of thy peace, and makest them to sit down at thy Table. We entreat thee of thy great mercy to perfect in them the good work thou hast begun, that they, being defended by thy fatherly hand, and strengthened with might by thy Spirit, may be enabled to keep this covenant without spot, unrebukable, until the day of our Lord Jesus Christ. *Amen.*

OUR Father, who art in heaven, Hallowed be thy name; Thy kingdom come; Thy will be done; In earth as it is in heaven. Give us this day our daily bread. And forgive us our trespasses, As we forgive them that trespass against us. And lead us not into temptation; But deliver us from evil: For thine is the kingdom, The power, and the glory, For ever and ever. Amen.

¶ *After which may follow this Ascription of Praise.*

NOW unto him that is able to keep you from falling and to present you faultless before the presence of his glory with exceeding joy; to the only wise God our Saviour, be glory and majesty, dominion and power, both now and ever. *Amen.*

¶ *A public service for the Reception to Full Communion and the Confirmation of Baptized Persons is not to be regarded as an invariable condition of full membership; the occasions when it may be necessary or proper to follow another manner being left to the prudence and judgement of the office-bearers of the Church.*

APPENDIX

A PROFESSION OF FAITH

Instead of the short form of the Apostles' Creed, this question, as equivalent thereto, may be used.

DO you now for yourselves profess the Christian faith in which you were baptized?

CONCLUSIONS

Which may be used after the Lord's Prayer and in place of the Ascription of Praise.

I

The Minister may say to all that have been received,

IN the name of the Lord Jesus Christ, I receive and welcome you to the fellowship of his Table, and to all the privileges of full communion with the Church of Christ.

And the blessing of God Almighty, Father, Son, and Holy Spirit, be upon you, and remain with you always. *Amen.*

II

Where it is the custom, all may covenant together as followeth.

The Minister shall first say to them that have been received,

BELOVED of the Lord, baptized in the name of the Father, and of the Son, and of the Holy Ghost, you have already confessed the faith of Christ before his people, and given yourselves to God in the everlasting covenant of grace. And now that you cordially join yourselves with this Church of Christ, you promise to wait diligently upon its ordinances, to study its peace and prosperity, to pray and labour for its edification and fruitfulness, and to live with this people of God in Christian fellowship. Do you so promise?

Answer. I do.

The members of the Church shall then stand, and the Minister shall say,

WE the members of this Church, do affectionately welcome you into this household of faith. We pledge to you our sympathy, our help, and our prayers, that you may evermore increase in the knowledge and love of God. We trust that by his grace we may all walk worthy of the calling wherewith we are called, with all lowliness and meekness, forbearing one another in love; giving diligence to keep the unity of the spirit in the bond of peace, and remembering all Christ's sheep that wander and go astray, that they may be gathered and brought home to his fold. God grant that, serving and being served, we may together be prepared for the perfect fellowship of the saints above.

Here may the Minister give to each of the newly-received the right hand of welcome.

Then may follow a Benediction.

AN ORDER FOR

THE BAPTISM OF SUCH AS ARE OF RIPER YEARS

AND ABLE TO ANSWER FOR THEMSELVES

¶ *The Minister may, before the administration of the Sacrament, give instruction touching its nature and meaning, using, if he will, the following Exhortation.*

Hear the words of the Gospel of our Lord and Saviour according to St. Matthew.

ALL power is given unto me in heaven and in earth. Go ye therefore, and teach all nations, baptizing them in the name of the Father, and of the Son, and of the Holy Spirit: teaching them to observe all things whatsoever I have commanded you: and lo, I am with you alway, even unto the end of the world.

St. Peter also, on the day of Pentecost, called upon the people, saying, Repent, and be baptized, every one of you, in the name of Jesus Christ, for the remission of sins, and ye shall receive the gift of the Holy Spirit. For the promise is unto you, and to your children, and to all that are afar off, even as many as the Lord our God shall call.

Doubt ye not, therefore, but earnestly believe that he will number among his people these persons (*or* this person), coming unto him by faith, that he will grant *them* remission of their sins, and bestow upon *them* the Holy Spirit; that he will give *them* the blessing of eternal life, and make *them* partakers of his everlasting kingdom.

THE BAPTISM

¶ *The Minister, standing at the Font, shall say to the persons to be baptized.*

WELL-BELOVED, who are come hither desiring to profess your faith in Christ and to receive Holy Baptism, you have heard that our Lord Jesus Christ hath promised in his Word to grant forgiveness of sins and his Holy Spirit unto all that repent and turn unto him; which promise, he, for his part, will most surely keep and perform.

Wherefore, after this promise made by Christ, you must also faithfully, for your part, promise in the presence of God and this congregation to follow Christ as your Lord and Master, turning away from what he forbiddeth and doing whatsoever he commandeth.

¶ *And he shall ask each of them, severally, these questions following.*

DO you believe in God the Father Almighty, Maker of heaven, and earth; and in Jesus Christ, his only Son our Lord, who was born into the world, and who suffered for us; and in the Holy Ghost, the Holy Catholic Church, the Communion of Saints, the Forgiveness of sins, and the Life everlasting?

Answer. I do.

WILL you then endeavour to keep God's holy will and commandments, and to walk in the same all the days of your life?

Answer. I will.

DO you promise to make diligent use of the means of grace, and in all things to seek earnestly the peace and welfare of the Church of God?

Answer. I do so promise, God being my helper.

¶ *Then shall follow this Prayer.*

WE beseech thee, O Lord, that it may please thee to receive, and to sanctify with thy Spirit, these persons (*or* this thy servant) now to be baptized according to thy Word; that *they* may obtain the fullness of thy grace, and ever remain in the number of thy faithful children; through Jesus Christ our Lord. *Amen.*

¶ *Then shall the persons presenting themselves for Baptism kneel, and the Minister shall pour or sprinkle water upon their heads severally, calling each by name, and saying,*

N. I BAPTIZE thee In the name of the Father, and of the Son, and of the Holy Ghost. Amen.

Then shall the Minister say,

WE receive *these persons* into the congregation of Christ's flock, that as living members (*or* a living member) of the same, *they* may be made *partakers* of the fullness of divine grace, and grow up into union with Christ who is our Saviour and Lord.

THE CONFIRMATION

¶ *Then shall the Minister say,*

Let us pray.

ALMIGHTY and everlasting God, strengthen, we beseech thee, *these* thy *servants* with the Holy Spirit the Comforter, and daily increase in *them* thy manifold gifts of grace; the spirit of wisdom and understanding; the spirit of counsel and strength; the spirit of knowledge and true godliness; fill *them,* O Lord, with the spirit of thy holy fear; and keep *them* in thy mercy unto life eternal; through Jesus Christ our Lord. *Amen.*

¶ *Then the Minister* (*laying his hand, if such be his discretion, upon the head of every one in order kneeling before him*) *shall say,*

THE God of grace, who hath called thee unto his eternal glory by Jesus Christ, confirm thee to the end, that thou mayest be blameless in the day of our Lord Jesus Christ. *Amen.*

Or else,

DEFEND, O Lord, this thy servant with thy heavenly grace, that *he* may continue thine for ever; and daily increase in thy Holy Spirit more and more, until *he* come unto thy everlasting kingdom. *Amen.*

¶ *Then shall the Minister say,*

Let us pray.

ALMIGHTY God, our heavenly Father, we give thee hearty thanks and praise that thou hast not withheld thy loving kindness from *these* thy *servants,* but hast given *them* shelter within the covenant of thy peace, and makest *them* to sit down at thy Table. We entreat thee of thy great mercy to perfect in *them* the good work thou hast begun; that *they* being defended by thy fatherly hand, and strengthened with power through thy Spirit in the inward man, may be enabled to keep his covenant without spot, unrebukable, until the day of the appearing of the Lord Jesus Christ. *Amen.*

And all shall say together the Lord's Prayer.

¶ *After which may follow this Blessing.*

THE Lord bless you, and keep you: the Lord make his face to shine upon you, and be gracious unto you: the Lord lift up his countenance upon you, and give you peace. *Amen.*

¶ *Where it is desirable a candidate may be dipped in the water.*

¶ *Forasmuch as by this rite there is admission to full membership in the Church, the essential parts of the two foregoing Orders are included in this Order.*

A PROFESSION OF FAITH

Instead of the short form of the Apostles' Creed, this question, as equivalent thereto, may be used.

DO you believe in God, Father, Son, and Holy Spirit; and do you confess the Lord Jesus Christ as your Saviour and Lord?

AN ORDER FOR

THE RECEPTION OF COMMUNICANTS FROM OTHER CHURCHES

I

¶ *When Communicants from other Churches are received it is fitting that the Minister should read their names, and, bidding them stand forth, should say to them,*

IN the name of the Lord Jesus Christ we bid you welcome to the fellowship of this Church.

And he may bless them, saying,

MAY the almighty God order your days in his peace, and grant you the gifts of his blessing. *Amen.*

II

¶ *Where it is the custom that all should covenant together at such a time, the following Order may be used.*

¶ *The Minister shall call them that are to be received by their names, and, bidding them stand forth, he shall say to them,*

DEARLY beloved, you have already confessed the faith of Christ before his people, and given yourselves to God in the everlasting covenant of grace. Now you come to join yourselves with this Church of Christ. In doing so, you undertake to wait diligently upon its ordinances, to study its peace and prosperity, to pray and labour for its edification and fruitfulness, and to live with this people of God in Christian fellowship. Do you so promise?

Answer. I do so promise, God helping me.

Then the Minister may bid all the members of the Church to stand, and speaking for them, he shall say,

IN the name of the Lord Jesus, we, the members of this Church, do welcome you into its fellowship and covenant. We pledge to you our sympathy, our help, and our prayers, that you may evermore increase in the knowledge and love of God. We trust that by his grace we may all walk worthy of the calling wherewith we are called, with all lowliness and meekness, forbearing one another in love; giving diligence to keep the unity of the spirit in the bond of peace, and remembering all Christ's sheep that wander and go astray, that they may be gathered and brought home to his fold. God grant that, serving and being served, we may be prepared while we dwell together on earth for the fellowship of the saints in heaven.

And he may bless them all, saying,

MAY the almighty God order your days in his peace, and grant you the gifts of his blessing. *Amen.*

AN ORDER FOR
THE SOLEMNIZATION OF MATRIMONY

¶ *At the time appointed for the Solemnization of Matrimony, the persons to be married, standing together, the man on the right and the woman on the left, the Minister shall say,*

THE INTRODUCTION

DEARLY beloved, we are gathered here in the presence of God to join together this man and this woman in Holy Matrimony; which is an honourable estate, ordained of God unto the fulfilling and perfecting of the love of man and woman in mutual honour and forbearance; and therefore it is not by any to be taken in hand lightly, or thoughtlessly, but reverently, discreetly, soberly, and in the fear of God.

Into which holy estate these two persons present come now to be joined.

Therefore if any man can show just cause, why they may not lawfully be joined together, let him now speak, or else hereafter for ever hold his peace.

¶ *Then speaking to the persons that are to be married the Minister shall say,*

I REQUIRE and charge you both, before the great God the Searcher of all hearts, that if either of you know any impediment, why ye may not lawfully be joined together in Marriage, ye do now confess it. For be ye well assured that so many as are joined together otherwise than as God's Word doth allow, are not joined together by God; neither is their union blessed by him.

THE MARRIAGE

¶ *If no impediment be alleged, then shall the Minister say unto the man,*

N. WILT thou have this woman to be thy wedded wife, to live together after God's ordinance in the holy estate of Matrimony? Wilt thou love her, comfort her, honour and keep her, in sickness and in health? and, forsaking all other, keep thee only unto her, so long as ye both shall live?

The man shall answer,

I will.

Then shall the Minister say unto the woman,

N. WILT thou have this man to be thy wedded husband, to live together after God's ordinance in the holy estate of Matrimony? Wilt thou love him, comfort him, honour and keep him, in sickness and in health? and, forsaking all other, keep thee only unto him, so long as ye both shall live?

The woman shall answer,

I will.

Then shall the Minister say,

Who giveth this woman to be married to this man?

Then shall they plight their troth to each other in this manner.

The Minister shall cause the man with his right hand to take the woman by her right hand and to say after him as followeth.

I, N. take thee N. to be my wedded wife, to have and to hold from this day forward, for better, for worse; for richer, for poorer; in sickness and in health; to love and to cherish, till death us do part, according to God's holy ordinance; and thereto I plight thee my troth.

Then shall they loose their hands; and the woman with her right hand taking the man by his right hand shall likewise say after the Minister,

I, N. take thee N. to be my wedded husband, to have and to hold from this day forward, for better, for worse; for richer, for poorer; in sickness and in health; to love and to cherish, till death us do part, according to God's holy ordinance; and thereto I plight thee my troth.

Then they shall again loose their hands; and the man shall give to the woman a ring, putting it upon the fourth finger of her left hand; and holding it there, shall say after the Minister,

THIS ring I give thee in token of the covenant made this day between us: In the name of the Father, and of the Son, and of the Holy Spirit. Amen.

¶ *Then may the man and the woman kneel down; but the People shall remain standing. And the Minister shall say,*

Let us pray.

O ETERNAL God, Creator and Preserver of all mankind, giver of all spiritual grace, the author of everlasting life: Send thy blessing upon these thy servants, this man and this woman, whom we bless in thy name; that, living faithfully together, they may surely perform and keep the vow and covenant betwixt them made; and may ever remain in perfect love and peace together, and live according to thy law; through Jesus Christ our Lord. *Amen.*

Then shall the Minister join their right hands together, and say,

Those whom God hath joined together let not man put asunder.

Then shall the Minister speak unto the People.

FORASMUCH as N. and N. have consented together in holy wedlock, and have witnessed the same before God and this company, and thereto have given and pledged their troth either to other, and have declared the same by giving and receiving of a ring, and by joining of hands; I pronounce that they be man and wife together, In the name of the Father, and of the Son, and of the Holy Ghost. Amen.

And the Minister shall add this Blessing.

GOD the Father, Son, and Holy Spirit, bless, preserve, and keep you; the Lord mercifully with his favour look upon you;

and so fill you with all spiritual benediction and grace, that ye may so live together in this life, that in the world to come ye may have life everlasting. *Amen.*

Or this.

THE Lord bless you, and keep you: the Lord make his face to shine upon you, and be gracious unto you: the Lord lift up his countenance upon you, and give you peace. *Amen.*

THE BLESSING OF THE MARRIAGE

¶ *While the marriage of the man and the woman needs nothing further to make it a valid marriage, it is desirable that the sons and daughters of the Church should seek further the divine blessing upon the union in the manner following.*

First Form of Blessing

¶ *This Psalm following shall be sung or said.*

Psalm 121

I WILL lift up mine eyes unto the hills, whence cometh my help.

My help cometh from the Lord, which made heaven and earth.

He will not suffer thy foot to be moved: he that keepeth thee will not slumber.

Behold, he that keepeth Israel shall neither slumber nor sleep.

The Lord is thy keeper: the Lord is thy shade upon thy right hand.

The sun shall not smite thee by day, nor the moon by night.

The Lord shall preserve thee from all evil: he shall preserve thy soul.

The Lord shall preserve thy going out and thy coming in from this time forth, and even for evermore.

Or this Psalm.

Psalm 37. 3-7.

TRUST in the Lord, and do good; so shalt thou dwell in the land, and verily thou shalt be fed.

Delight thyself also in the Lord; and he shall give thee the desires of thine heart.

Commit thy way unto the Lord; trust also in him; and he shall bring it to pass.

And he shall bring forth thy righteousness as the light, and thy judgement as the noon-day.

Rest in the Lord, and wait patiently for him.

¶ *The Psalm ended, the Minister standing, if it be convenient, at the Lord's Table, shall say,*

Let us pray.

Minister. Lord, have mercy upon us.
People. Christ, have mercy upon us.
Minister. Lord, have mercy upon us.

Minister. O Lord, save thy servant, and thy handmaid;

People. Who put their trust in thee.

Minister. O Lord, send them help from thy holy place;

People. And evermore defend them.

And the Minister shall continue as followeth.

O GOD, the Author and Giver of all good things, who hast consecrated this estate of Marriage, and made it holy: Let thy blessing, we beseech thee, descend and rest upon these thy servants, that they may dwell together in unity and love all the days of their life. Grant unto them health, prosperity, and peace. And above all things, we pray thee to enrich their souls with thy heavenly grace, that they may obey and serve thee, walking in the steps of Jesus Christ thy Son; that finally when the joys and sorrows, and all the good and evil of this passing world are ended, they may inherit thy promises and be made partakers of eternal peace; through Jesus Christ our Lord. *Amen.*

And all shall say together the Lord's Prayer.

OUR Father, who art in heaven, Hallowed be thy name; Thy kingdom come; Thy will be done; In earth as it is in heaven. Give us this day our daily bread. And forgive us our trespasses, As we forgive them that trespass against us. And lead us not into temptation; but deliver us from evil: For thine is the kingdom, The power, and the glory, For ever and ever. Amen.

¶ *Then shall the Minister say this Blessing over the man and the woman.*

ALMIGHTY God, the Father of our Lord Jesus Christ, Pour upon you the riches of his grace, sanctify and bless you, that ye may please him both in body and soul, and live together in holy love unto your lives' end. *Amen.*

¶ *And he shall dismiss those that are gathered together with this Blessing.*

THE peace of God, which passeth all understanding, keep your hearts and minds in the knowledge and love of God, and of his Son Jesus Christ our Lord; and the blessing of God Almighty, the Father, the Son, and the Holy Spirit, be amongst you and remain with you always. *Amen.*

Second Form of Blessing

¶ *If the newly-married are immediately to receive the Holy Communion this Psalm shall be sung or said while the Minister, with the man and the woman, goes to the Lord's Table.*

Psalm 121.

I WILL lift up mine eyes unto the hills, whence cometh my help.

My help cometh from the Lord, which made heaven and earth.

He will not suffer thy foot to be moved: he that keepeth thee will not slumber.

Behold, he that keepeth Israel shall neither slumber nor sleep.

The Lord is thy keeper; the Lord is thy shade upon thy right hand.

The sun shall not smite thee by day, nor the moon by night.

The Lord shall preserve thee from all evil; he shall preserve thy soul.

The Lord shall preserve thy going out and thy coming in from this time forth, and even for evermore.

Or this Psalm.

Psalm 37. 3-7.

TRUST in the Lord, and do good, so shalt thou dwell in the land, and verily thou shalt be fed.

Delight thyself also in the Lord; and he shall give thee the desires of thine heart.

Commit thy way unto the Lord; trust also in him; and he shall bring it to pass.

And he shall bring forth thy righteousness as the light, and thy judgement as the noonday.

Rest in the Lord, and wait patiently for him.

¶ *Then shall the Minister say,*

Let us pray.

O LORD God our Father, who hast taught us by thy Son that except we love one another as thou lovest us we cannot fulfil thy law: Grant that thy Holy Spirit may lead these thy servants in the way of love, joy, and peace even unto eternal life; through the same thy Son, who loved us and gave himself for us, Jesus Christ our Lord. *Amen.*

¶ *Then shall the Holy Scripture be read as followeth.*

The Epistle. Ephesians 3. 14-19.

FOR this cause I bow my knees unto the Father of our Lord Jesus Christ, of whom the whole family in heaven and earth is named, that he would grant you, according to the riches of his glory, to be strengthened with might by his Spirit in the inner man; that Christ may dwell in your hearts by faith; that ye, being rooted and grounded in love, may be able to comprehend with all saints what is the breadth, and length, and depth, and height; and to know the love of Christ, which passeth knowledge, that ye might be filled with all the fullness of God.

Or else this.

1 Corinthians 13. 4-8.

LOVE suffereth long, and is kind; love envieth not; love vaunteth not itself, is not puffed up, doth not behave itself unseemly, seeketh not its own, is not easily provoked, thinketh no evil; rejoiceth not in unrighteousness, but rejoiceth in the truth; beareth all things, believeth all things, hopeth all things, endureth all things. Love never faileth.

The Gospel. St. John 15. 9-12.

AS the Father hath loved me, so have I loved you: continue ye in my love. If ye keep my commandments, ye shall abide in my love; even as I have kept my Father's commandments, and abide in his love. These things have I spoken unto you, that my joy might remain in you, and that your joy might be full. This is my commandment, That ye love one another, as I have loved you.

Or else this.

St. Matthew 19. 4-6.

JESUS answered and said unto the Pharisees, Have ye not read, that he which made them at the beginning made them male and female, and said, For this cause shall a man leave father and mother, and shall cleave to his wife: and they twain shall be one flesh? Wherefore they are no more twain, but one flesh. What therefore God hath joined together, let not man put asunder.

¶ *And the Minister may give an Address.*

¶ *Then shall he go on in the Order for Holy Communion. The Prayer* O God, the Author and Giver, *and the accompanying Blessing of the man and the woman, shall be said immediately before the Final Blessing.*

Third Form of Blessing

¶ *The Second Form may be followed as far as the Gospel (or the Address); and then, after general Thanksgiving and Intercession, the Prayer* O God, the Author and Giver, *may be said, and the Service may end with two Blessings as in the First Form.*

A PRAYER

Which may be used after the inquiry concerning impediment, and before the Marriage.

ALMIGHTY God, our heavenly Father, from whom cometh down every good and perfect gift; Lift thou the light of thy countenance, we beseech thee, upon us thy children. May thy blessing which maketh rich and addeth no sorrow, rest upon these thy servants, who are now about to be united in holy Matrimony according to thine own institution and ordinance. Grant that, acknowledging thee, and seeking to please thee in this and all things, they may be made exceeding glad with thy countenance, and may enjoy thy loving kindness which is better than life; through Jesus Christ our Lord. *Amen.*

¶ *The laws respecting the Solemnization of Matrimony, whether by publishing the banns in Churches, or by license, being different in the several Provinces, every Minister is required to know and observe the laws of his own Province.*

¶ *And when the banns are published, it shall be in the following form:* I publish the banns of marriage between N. of . . . . , and N. of . . . . , If any of you know just cause why these two persons should not be joined together in holy Matrimony, ye are to declare it. This is the first (second *or* third) time of asking.

THE VISITATION OF THE SICK

The following passages of Holy Scripture are suitable for use with a sick person.

1. Confidence in God: Psalms 27, 46, 91, 121; Proverbs 3. 11-26; Isaiah 26. 1-9; 40. 1-11; 40. 25 to end; Lamentations 3. 22-41; St. Matthew 6. 24 to end; Romans 8. 31 to end.

2. Answer to Prayer: Psalms 30, 34.

3. Prayer for Divine Aid: Psalms 43, 86, 143; St. James 5. 10 to end.

4. Penitence: Psalms 51, 130.

5. Praise and Thanksgiving: Psalms 103, 146; Isaiah 12.

6. God's Dealing with Man through Affliction: Job 33. 14-30; Hebrews 12. 1-11.

7. Christ our Example in Suffering: Isaiah 53; St. Matthew 26. 36-46; St. Luke 23. 27-49.

8. God's Call to Repentance and Faith; Isaiah 55.

9. The Beatitudes: St. Matthew 5. 1-12.

10. Watchfulness: St. Luke 12. 32-40.

11. Christ the Good Shepherd: Psalm 23; St. John 10. 1-18.

12. The Resurrection: St. John 20. 1-18; 20. 19 to end; 2 Corinthians 4. 13 to 5. 9.

13. Redemption: Romans 5. 1-11; 8. 18 to end; 1 St. John 1. 1-9.

14. Christian Love: 1 Corinthians 13.

15. Growth in Grace: Ephesians 3. 13 to end; 6. 10-20; Philippians 3. 7-14.

16. Patience in Suffering: St. James 5. 10 to end.

17. God's Love to Men: 1 St. John 3. 1-7; 4. 9 to end.

18. The Life of the World to come: Revelation 7. 9 to end; 21. 1-7; 21. 22 to end; 22. 1-5.

19. Our Lord's last Discourse before his Passion: St. John 14, 15, 16, 17.

20. Christian Hope on the Approach of Death: Deuteronomy 33. 27; Psalm 16. 9 to end; Psalm 23; St. John 3. 16; 2 Corinthians 4. 16 to 5. 1; Revelation 21. 4-7.

AN ORDER FOR

THE COMMUNION OF THE SICK

¶ *If a sick person be not able to come to the Church and yet be desirous to receive the Communion, it may be ministered to him in his house.*

¶ *Ordinarily it is much to be desired that there be some, beside the Minister, to communicate with the sick person.*

¶ *The Minister may celebrate the Holy Communion according to either form set down in this book, or else he may use the Order following.*

¶ *All things necessary being ready, the Minister shall begin with the Prayer for Grace, Epistle, and Gospel here following.*

The Prayer for Grace.

ALMIGHTY and immortal God, giver of life and health: We beseech thee to hear our prayers for this thy servant, that by thy blessing upon *him* and upon those who minister to *him, he* may be restored to health of body and mind, and give thanks to thee in thy holy Church; through Jesus Christ our Lord. *Amen.*

The Epistle. 2 Corinthians 1. 3-5.

BLESSED be God, even the Father of our Lord Jesus Christ, the Father of mercies, and the God of all comfort; who comforteth us in all our tribulation, that we may be able to comfort them which are in any trouble, by the comfort wherewith we ourselves are comforted of God. For as the sufferings of Christ abound in us, so our consolation also aboundeth by Christ.

The Gospel. St. John 10. 14, 15, 27-30.

I AM the good shepherd; and I know mine own, and mine own know me, even as the Father knoweth me, and I know the Father; and I lay down my life for the sheep. My sheep hear my voice, and I know them, and they follow me: and I give unto them eternal life; and they shall never perish, and no one shall pluck them out of my hand. My Father, which hath given them unto me, is greater than all; and no one is able to pluck them out of the Father's hand. I and the Father are one.

¶ *Here may be read the narrative of the institution of the Lord's Supper.* 1 *Corinthians* 11. 23-26.

I HAVE received of the Lord that which also I delivered unto you, That the Lord Jesus the same night in which he was betrayed took bread: and when he had given thanks, he brake it, and said, Take, eat: this is my body, which is broken for you: this do in remembrance of me. After the same manner also he took the cup, when he had supped, saying, This cup is the new testament in my blood: this do ye, as oft as ye drink it, in remembrance of me. For as often as ye eat this bread, and drink this cup, ye do shew the Lord's death till he come.

¶ *Then shall follow this Confession and Prayer for Pardon.*

WE confess to God, Father, Son, and Holy Spirit, and to all the company of heaven, and to one another, that we have sinned, in thought, word, and deed, and by omission, through our fault, our own fault, our own grievous fault; wherefore we pray Almighty God to have mercy upon us, to forgive us our sins, and to make clean our hearts within us.

MAY the almighty and merciful Lord grant us pardon, absolution, and remission of our sins. *Amen.*

¶ *Then shall the Minister say,*

Let us pray.

ALL glory and thanksgiving be unto thee, Almighty God, our heavenly Father, for that thou of thy tender mercy didst give thine only Son Jesus Christ to take our nature upon him and to suffer death upon the Cross for our redemption;

Who, the same night in which he was betrayed, took bread, and when he had given thanks, he brake it, and said, Take, eat; this is my Body which is broken for you;

this do in remembrance of me. After the same manner also he took the cup, saying, This cup is the new Covenant in my Blood; this do ye, as oft as ye drink it, in remembrance of me.

Not as we ought, but as we are able, do we bless thee for his holy incarnation, for his perfect life on earth, for his precious sufferings and death upon the Cross, for his glorious resurrection and ascension, and for the promise of his coming again.

And we most humbly beseech thee, O merciful Father, to look upon us as we do now make that memorial of his blessed sacrifice which he hath commanded us to make; and send down thy Holy Spirit to bless and consecrate these thine own gifts of bread and wine which we set before thee, that the bread which we break may be unto us the Communion of the Body of Christ, and the cup which we bless the Communion of the Blood of Christ; that we, receiving them, may by faith be made partakers of his Body and Blood, with all his benefits, to our spiritual nourishment and growth in grace, and to the glory of thy holy name. *Amen.*

OUR Father, who art in heaven, Hallowed be thy name; Thy kingdom come; Thy will be done; In earth as it is in heaven. Give us this day our daily bread. And forgive us our trespasses, As we forgive them that trespass against us. And lead us not into temptation; But deliver us from evil: For thine is the kingdom, The power, and the glory, For ever and ever. Amen.

¶ *Then shall the Minister break the Bread and lift the Cup.*

¶ *Then shall he and as many as may receive with him, partake of the Sacrament, the customary words being used at the delivery of the Bread and the Wine.*

¶ *Then shall follow Thanksgiving for Communion, Prayer for grace to persevere, and the Blessing.*

¶ *In case of extreme necessity the Minister may say the Prayer,* We most humbly beseech thee, O merciful Father; *and, immediately after the delivery of the Sacrament to the sick person, end with the Blessing.*

ORDERS FOR

THE BURIAL OF THE DEAD

¶ *Of the two Orders which follow either may be used at the House or at the Church (if there be a Service at the Church). But if there be two Services, the first will ordinarily be used at the House and the second at the Church.*

I

THE INTRODUCTION

¶ *When this Order is used at the House the Minister shall say one or more of the following Sentences.*

I AM the resurrection and the life, saith the Lord: he that believeth in me, though he were dead, yet shall he live: and whosoever liveth and believeth in me shall never die. *St. John* 11. 25, 26.

I KNOW that my Redeemer liveth, and that he shall stand up at the last upon the earth: whom I shall see for myself, and mine eyes shall behold, and not another. *Job* 19. 25, 27.

WE brought nothing into this world, and it is certain we can carry nothing out. The Lord gave, and the Lord hath taken away; blessed be the name of the Lord.

1 Timothy 6. 7. *Job* 1. 21.

THE eternal God is thy refuge, and underneath are the everlasting arms.

Deuteronomy 33. 27.

NEITHER death, nor life, nor angels, nor principalities, nor powers, nor things present, nor things to come, nor height, nor depth, nor any other creature, shall be able to separate us from the love of God, which is in Christ Jesus our Lord. *Romans* 8. 38, 39.

WHETHER we live, we live unto the Lord; and whether we die, we die unto the Lord: whether we live therefore, or die, we are the Lord's. For to this end Christ both died, and rose, and revived, that he might be Lord both of the dead and living.

Romans 14. 8, 9.

BLESSED are they that mourn: for they shall be comforted. *St. Matthew* 5. 4.

LET not your heart be troubled: ye believe in God, believe also in me. In my Father's house are many mansions. *St. John* 14. 1, 2.

At the Burial of a Child.

HE shall feed his flock like a shepherd: he shall gather the lambs with his arm, and carry them in his bosom. *Isaiah* 40. 11.

JESUS said, Suffer the little children to come unto me, and forbid them not: for of such is the kingdom of heaven.

St. Mark 10. 14.

¶ *When this Order is used at the Church, the Minister shall meet the body at the door, and shall go before it into the Church. In the meantime a Psalm or Hymn may be sung; then shall the Minister say one or more of the Sentences above. But if no Psalm or Hymn be sung, the Minister may say the Sentences as he goes before the body into the Church.*

THE PSALMS

¶ *Then shall be read one or more of the Psalms following* (*No.* 23 *or No.* 103 *being suitable at the Burial of a Child*).

Psalm 23.

THE Lord is my shepherd; I shall not want.

He maketh me to lie down in green pastures: he leadeth me beside the still waters.

He restoreth my soul: he leadeth me in the paths of righteousness for his name's sake.

Yea, though I walk through the valley of the shadow of death, I will fear no evil: for thou art with me; thy rod and thy staff they comfort me.

Thou preparest a table before me in the presence of mine enemies: thou anointest my head with oil; my cup runneth over.

Surely goodness and mercy shall follow me all the days of my life: and I will dwell in the house of the Lord for ever.

Psalm 39. 4-13.

LORD, make me to know mine end, and the measure of my days, what it is; that I may know how frail I am.

Behold, thou hast made my days as an handbreadth; and mine age is as nothing before thee: verily every man at his best state is altogether vanity.

Surely every man walketh in a vain shew: surely they are disquieted in vain: he heapeth up riches, and knoweth not who shall gather them.

And now, Lord, what wait I for? my hope is in thee.

Deliver me from all my transgressions: make me not the reproach of the foolish.

I was dumb, I opened not my mouth; because thou didst it.

Remove thy stroke away from me: I am consumed by the blow of thine hand.

When thou with rebukes dost correct man for iniquity, thou makest his beauty to consume away like a moth: surely every man is vanity.

Hear my prayer, O Lord, and give ear unto my cry; hold not thy peace at my tears.

For I am a stranger with thee, and a sojourner, as all my fathers were.

O spare me, that I may recover strength, before I go hence, and be no more.

Psalm 90. 1-6, 10, 12, 14-17.

LORD, thou hast been our dwelling place in all generations.

Before the mountains were brought forth, or ever thou hadst formed the earth and the world, even from everlasting to everlasting, thou art God.

Thou turnest man to destruction; and sayest, Return, ye children of men.

For a thousand years in thy sight are but as yesterday when it is past, and as a watch in the night.

Thou carriest them away as with a flood; they are as a sleep: in the morning they are like grass which groweth up.

In the morning it flourisheth, and groweth up; in the evening it is cut down, and withereth.

The days of our years are threescore years and ten; and if by reason of strength they be fourscore years, yet is their strength labour and sorrow; for it is soon cut off, and we fly away.

So teach us to number our days, that we may apply our hearts unto wisdom.

O satisfy us early with thy mercy; that we may rejoice and be glad all our days.

Make us glad according to the days wherein thou hast afflicted us, and the years wherein we have seen evil.

Let thy work appear unto thy servants, and thy glory unto their children.

And let the beauty of the Lord our God be upon us: and establish thou the work of our hands upon us; yea, the work of our hands establish thou it.

Psalm 103. 13-17.

LIKE as a father pitieth his children, so the Lord pitieth them that fear him.

For he knoweth our frame; he remembereth that we are dust.

As for man, his days are as grass: as a flower of the field, so he flourisheth.

For the wind passeth over it, and it is gone; and the place thereof shall know it no more.

But the mercy of the Lord is from everlasting to everlasting upon them that fear him, and his righteousness unto children's children.

Psalm 116. 1-9.

I LOVE the Lord, because he hath heard my voice and my supplications.

Because he hath inclined his ear unto me, therefore will I call upon him as long as I live.

The sorrows of death compassed me, and the pains of hell gat hold upon me; I found trouble and sorrow.

Then called I upon the name of the Lord; O Lord, I beseech thee, deliver my soul.

Gracious is the Lord, and righteous; yea, our God is merciful.

The Lord preserveth the simple: I was brought low, and he helped me.

Return unto thy rest, O my soul; for the Lord hath dealt bountifully with thee.

For thou hast delivered my soul from death, mine eyes from tears, and my feet from falling.

I will walk before the Lord in the land of the living.

Psalm 121.

I WILL lift up mine eyes unto the hills, from whence cometh my help.

My help cometh from the Lord, which made heaven and earth.

He will not suffer thy foot to be moved: he that keepeth thee will not slumber.

Behold, he that keepeth Israel shall neither slumber nor sleep.

The Lord is thy keeper: the Lord is thy shade upon thy right hand.

The sun shall not smite thee by day, nor the moon by night.

The Lord shall preserve thee from all evil: he shall preserve thy soul.

The Lord shall preserve thy going out and thy coming in from this time forth, and even for evermore.

Psalm 130.

OUT of the depths have I cried unto thee, O Lord.

Lord, hear my voice: let thine ears be attentive to the voice of my supplications.

If thou, Lord, shouldest mark iniquities, O Lord, who shall stand?

But there is forgiveness with thee, that thou mayest be feared.

I wait for the Lord, my soul doth wait, and in his word do I hope.

My soul waiteth for the Lord more than they that watch for the morning: I say more than they that watch for the morning.

Let Israel hope in the Lord: for with the Lord there is mercy, and with him is plenteous redemption.

And he shall redeem Israel from all his iniquities.

Psalm 139. 1-12, 17, 18.

O LORD, thou hast searched me, and known me.

Thou knowest my downsitting and mine uprising, thou understandest my thought afar off.

Thou compassest my path and my lying down, and art acquainted with all my ways.

For there is not a word in my tongue, but, lo, O Lord, thou knowest it altogether.

Thou hast beset me behind and before,

and laid thine hand upon me. Such knowledge is too wonderful for me; it is high, I cannot attain unto it.

Whither shall I go from thy spirit? or whither shall I flee from thy presence?

If I ascend up into heaven, thou art there: if I make my bed in hell, behold, thou art there.

If I take the wings of the morning, and dwell in the uttermost parts of the sea;

Even there shall thy hand lead me, and thy right hand shall hold me.

If I say, Surely the darkness shall cover me; even the night shall be light about me.

Yea, the darkness hideth not from thee: but the night shineth as the day: the darkness and the light are both alike to thee.

How precious are thy thoughts unto me, O God! how great is the sum of them!

If I should count them, they are more in number than the sand: when I awake, I am still with thee.

THE LESSON

¶ *Then shall be read one of the Lessons following.*

1 Corinthians 15. 20-22, 35-38, 42-44, 50, 53-58.

NOW is Christ risen from the dead, and become the first-fruits of them that slept. For since by man came death, by man came also the resurrection of the dead. For as in Adam all die, even so in Christ shall all be made alive.

But some man will say, How are the dead raised up? and with what body do they come? Thou fool, that which thou sowest is not quickened, except it die: and that which thou sowest, thou sowest not that body that shall be, but bare grain, it may chance of wheat, or of some other grain: but God giveth it a body as it hath pleased him, and to every seed his own body.

So also is the resurrection of the dead. It is sown in corruption; it is raised in incorruption: it is sown in dishonour; it is raised in glory: it is sown in weakness; it is raised in power: it is sown a natural body; it is raised a spiritual body. There is a natural body, and there is a spiritual body.

Now this I say, brethren, that flesh and blood cannot inherit the kingdom of God; neither doth corruption inherit incorruption. For this corruptible must put on incorruption, and this mortal must put on immortality. So when this corruptible shall have put on incorruption, and this mortal shall have put on immortality, then shall be brought to pass the saying that is written, Death is swallowed up in victory. O death, where is thy sting? O grave, where is thy victory? The sting of death is sin; and the strength of sin is the law. But thanks be to God, which giveth us the victory through our Lord Jesus Christ. Therefore, my beloved brethren, be ye steadfast, unmoveable, always abounding in the work of the Lord, forasmuch as ye know that your labour is not in vain in the Lord.

Romans 8. 31-35, 37-39.

WHAT shall we then say to these things? If God be for us, who can be against us? He that spared not his own Son, but delivered him up for us all, how shall he not with him also freely give us all things? Who shall lay any thing to the charge of God's elect? It is God that justifieth. Who is he that condemneth? It is Christ that died, yea rather, that is risen again, who is even at the right hand of God, who also maketh intercession for us. Who shall separate us from the love of Christ? shall tribulation, or distress, or persecution, or famine, or nakedness, or peril, or sword? Nay, in all these things we are more than conquerors through him that loved us. For I am persuaded, that neither death, nor life, nor angels, nor principalities, nor powers, nor things present, nor things to come, nor height, nor depth, nor any other creature, shall be able to separate us from the love of God, which is in Christ Jesus our Lord.

1 St. Peter 1. 3-9.

BLESSED be the God and Father of our Lord Jesus Christ, which according to his abundant mercy hath begotten us again unto a living hope by the resurrection of Jesus Christ from the dead, to an inheritance incorruptible, and undefiled, and that fadeth not away, reserved in heaven for you, who are kept by the power of God through faith unto salvation ready to be revealed in the last time. Wherein ye greatly rejoice, though now for a season, if need be, ye are in heaviness through manifold temptations: that the trial of your faith, being much more precious than of gold that perisheth, though it be tried with fire, might be found unto praise and honour and glory at the appearing of Jesus Christ: whom having not seen, ye love; in whom, though now ye see him not, yet believing, ye rejoice with joy unspeakable and full of glory: receiving the end of your faith, even the salvation of your souls.

Revelation 7. 9-17.

AFTER this I beheld, and, lo, a great multitude, which no man could number, of all nations, and kindreds, and people, and tongues, stood before the throne, and before the Lamb, clothed with white robes, and palms in their hands; and cried with a loud voice, saying, Salvation to our God which sitteth upon the throne, and unto the Lamb. And all the angels stood round about the throne, and about the elders and the four beasts, and fell before the throne on their faces, and worshipped God, saying, Amen: Blessing, and glory, and wisdom, and thanksgiving, and honour, and power, and might, be unto our God for ever and ever. Amen. And one of the elders answered, saying unto me, What are these which are arrayed in white robes? and whence came they? And I said unto him, Sir, thou knowest. And he said to me, These are they which came out of great tribulation, and have washed their robes, and made them white in the blood of the Lamb. Therefore are they before the throne of God, and serve him day and night in his temple: and he that sitteth on the throne shall dwell among them. They shall hunger no more, neither thirst any more; neither shall the sun light on them, nor any heat. For the Lamb which is in the midst of the throne shall feed them, and shall lead them unto living fountains of waters: and God shall wipe away all tears from their eyes.

Revelation 21. 1-4; 22. 1-5.

AND I saw a new heaven and a new earth: for the first heaven and the first earth were passed away; and there was no more sea. And I John saw the holy city, new Jerusalem, coming down from God out of heaven, prepared as a bride adorned for her husband. And I heard a great voice out of heaven saying, Behold, the tabernacle of God is with men, and he will dwell with them, and they shall be his people, and God himself shall be with them, and be their God. And God shall wipe away all tears from their eyes; and there shall be no more death, neither sorrow, nor crying, neither shall there be any more pain: for the former things are passed away.

And he shewed me a pure river of water of life, clear as crystal, proceeding out of the throne of God and of the Lamb. In the midst of the street of it, and on either side of the river, was there the tree of life, which bare twelve manner of fruits, and yielded her fruit every month: and the leaves of the tree were for the healing of the nations. And there shall be no more curse: but the throne of God and of the Lamb shall be in it; and his servants shall serve him: and they shall see his face; and his name shall be in their foreheads. And there shall be no night there; and they need no candle, neither light of the sun; for the Lord God giveth them light: and they shall reign for ever and ever.

At the Burial of a Child.

St. Matthew 18. 1-5, 10, 14.

AT the same time came the disciples unto Jesus, saying, Who is the greatest in the kingdom of heaven? And Jesus called a little child unto him, and set him in the midst of them, and said, Verily I say unto you, Except ye be converted, and become as little children, ye shall not enter into the kingdom of heaven. Whosoever therefore shall humble himself as this little child, the same is greatest in the kingdom of heaven. And whoso shall receive one such little child in my name receiveth me.

Take heed that ye despise not one of these little ones; for I say unto you, That in heaven their angels do always behold the face of my Father which is in heaven.

Even so it is not the will of your Father which is in heaven, that one of these little ones should perish.

St. Mark 10. 13-16.

AND they brought young children to him, that he should touch them: and his disciples rebuked those that brought them. But when Jesus saw it, he was much displeased, and said unto them, Suffer the little children to come unto me, and forbid them not: for of such is the kingdom of God. Verily I say unto you, Whosoever shall not receive the kingdom of God as a little child, he shall not enter therein. And he took them up in his arms, put his hands upon them, and blessed them.

THE PRAYERS

¶ *Then shall follow Prayers, the Minister using, if he will, one or more of the Prayers set down here; and the Lord's Prayer shall be said also, with the Blessing.*

For the Divine Pity.

ALMIGHTY God, the Fountain of all wisdom, who knowest our necessities before we ask and our ignorance in asking: We beseech thee to have compassion upon our infirmities; and those things, which for our unworthiness we dare not, and for our blindness we cannot ask, vouchsafe to give us, for the worthiness of thy Son, Jesus Christ our Lord. *Amen.*

For Redemption in Christ.

ALMIGHTY and everlasting God, who of thy tender love towards mankind hast sent thy Son our Saviour Jesus Christ to take upon him our flesh, and to suffer death upon the Cross, that all mankind should follow the example of his great humility: Mercifully grant, that we may both follow the example of his patience, and also be made partakers of his resurrection; through the same Jesus Christ our Lord. *Amen.*

For the Bereaved.

O HEAVENLY Father, whose blessed Son Jesus Christ did weep at the grave of Lazarus his friend: Look, we beseech thee, with compassion upon those who are now in sorrow and affliction; comfort them, O God, with thy gracious consolations; make them to know that all things work together for good to them that love thee; and grant them evermore sure trust and confidence in thy fatherly care; through the same Jesus Christ our Lord. *Amen.*

ALMIGHTY God, Father of all mercies and giver of all comfort: Deal graciously, we pray thee, with those who mourn, that casting every care on thee, they may know the consolation of thy love; through Jesus Christ our Lord. *Amen.*

For Resignation.

O LORD God, our heavenly Father, who alone art the author and the disposer of our life, from whom our spirits have come, and to whom they shall return: We acknowledge thy sovereign power and right both to give and to take away, as seemeth good in thy sight; and we most humbly beseech thee, that unto all thy righteous dealings we may yield ourselves with due resignation and patience; being assured that though we understand not the mystery of thy ways, yet always in faithfulness, O Lord, dost thou afflict us, and for thy mercy's sake; through Jesus Christ our Lord. *Amen.*

For the Right Use of Affliction.

O GOD, whose days are without end, and whose mercies cannot be numbered: Make us deeply sensible of the shortness and uncertainty of human life, and let thy Holy Spirit lead us through this present world in holiness and righteousness all the days of our life; that, when we shall have served thee in our generation, we may be gathered unto our fathers, having the testimony of a good conscience; in the communion of thy holy Church; in the confidence of a certain faith; in the comfort of a reasonable, religious, and holy hope; in favour with thee our God; and in perfect charity with the world. All which we ask through Jesus Christ our Lord. *Amen.*

For Grace to Imitate the Righteous Dead.

O ALMIGHTY God, who hast knit together thine elect in one communion and fellowship in the mystical body of thy Son Christ our Lord: Grant us grace so to follow thy blessed saints in all virtuous and godly living, that we may come to those unspeakable joys, which thou hast prepared for them that unfeignedly love thee; through Jesus Christ our Lord. *Amen.*

ALMIGHTY and everliving God, we yield unto thee most high praise and hearty thanks for the wonderful grace and virtue declared in all thy saints, who have been the choice vessels of thy favour, and the lights of the world in their several generations; most humbly beseeching thee to give us grace so to follow the example of their steadfastness in thy faith, and obedience to thy holy commandments, that we may hold fast to them by the pure bonds of thy holy service, and hereafter may be united with them in thy heavenly kingdom; through Jesus Christ our Lord. *Amen.*

For Endurance to the End.

O GOD, thou King, eternal, immortal, and invisible, the blessed and only Potentate: May we, who cannot see thee with the eye of flesh, behold thee steadfastly with the eye of faith, that we may not faint under the manifold trials and temptations of this mortal life, but endure as seeing thee who art invisible; and grant that having fulfilled thy will upon earth, we may behold thy face in heaven, and be made partakers of those things which thou hast promised to them who love thy Son Jesus Christ our Lord, and wait his appearing; for whose sake we beseech thee to hear us; and unto whom, with thee the Father and the Holy Spirit, we ascribe all glory and praise, for ever and ever. *Amen.*

For the Divine Help.

ALMIGHTY God, give us grace that we may cast away the works of darkness and put upon us the armour of light, now in the time of this mortal life, in which thy Son Jesus Christ came to visit us in great humility; that in the last day, when he shall come again in his glorious majesty to judge both the quick and the dead, we may rise to the life immortal; through him who reigneth with thee and the Holy Spirit, now and ever. *Amen.*

O LORD, support us all the day long of this troublous life, until the shadows lengthen and the evening comes, and the busy world is hushed, and the fever of life is over, and our work is done. Then of thy tender mercy grant us a safe lodging, and a holy rest, and peace at the last; through Jesus Christ our Lord. *Amen.*

ALMIGHTY and everlasting God, who art always more ready to hear than we to pray, and art wont to give more than either we desire, or deserve: Pour down upon us the abundance of thy mercy; forgiving us those things whereof our conscience is afraid, and giving us those good things which we are not worthy to ask, but through the merits and mediation of Jesus Christ, thy Son, our Lord. *Amen.*

At the Burial of a Child.

O HEAVENLY Father, whose face the angels of the little ones do always behold in heaven: Grant us steadfastly to believe that this little child hath been taken into the safe keeping of thine eternal love; through Jesus Christ our Lord. *Amen.*

O GOD, whose ways are hidden and thy works most wonderful, who makest nothing in vain, and lovest all that thou hast made: Comfort thou thy servants whose hearts are sore smitten and oppressed; and grant that they may so love and serve thee in this life, that together with this thy child, they may obtain the fullness of thy promises in the world to come; through Jesus Christ our Lord. *Amen.*

THE LORD'S PRAYER

OUR Father, who art in heaven, Hallowed be thy name; Thy kingdom come; Thy will be done; In earth as it is in heaven. Give us this day our daily bread. And forgive us our trespasses, As we forgive them that trespass against us. And lead us not into temptation; But deliver us from evil: For thine is the kingdom, The power, and the glory, For ever and ever. Amen.

THE BLESSING

THE peace of God which passeth all understanding, keep your hearts and minds in the knowledge and love of God, and of his Son Jesus Christ our Lord: and the blessing of God Almighty, the Father, the Son, and the Holy Spirit, be amongst you and remain with you always. *Amen.*

II

THE INTRODUCTION

¶ *When this Order is used at the Church, the Minister shall meet the body at the door, and shall go before it into the Church. In the meantime a Psalm or Hymn may be sung.*

¶ *Then shall be said one of the Prayers following. But when the Order is used at the House the Service shall begin with the Prayer (or with a Psalm or Hymn, followed by the Prayer).*

ALMIGHTY God, our heavenly Father, who art our refuge and strength, and a very present help in time of trouble: Enable us, we pray thee, to put our trust in thee; and seeing that we have an high priest who is touched with the feeling of our infirmities, may we come boldly unto the throne of grace, that we may obtain mercy, and find grace to help in this time of need; through Jesus Christ our Lord. *Amen.*

ETERNAL God, our heavenly Father, who lovest us with an everlasting love and canst turn the shadow of death into the morning: Help us now to wait upon thee with reverent and submissive hearts, that as we read the words of eternal life, we through patience and comfort of the Scriptures may have hope, and be lifted above our darkness and distress into the light and peace of thy presence; through Jesus Christ our Lord. *Amen.*

O GOD, the Lord of life, the conqueror over death, our help in every time of trouble, who dost not willingly grieve nor afflict the children of men: Comfort us who mourn, and give us grace, in the presence of death, to worship thee the everliving, and while we follow the soul departed with love and hope, be enabled to put our whole trust in thy wonderful goodness and mercy; through Jesus Christ our Lord. Amen.

Here may follow one or more suitable Prayers.

THE WORD OF GOD

¶ *Then shall be read the Lesson following.*

1 Thessalonians 4. 13, 14, 18.

I WOULD not have you to be ignorant, brethren, concerning them which are asleep, that ye sorrow not, even as others which have no hope. For if we believe that Jesus died and rose again, even so them also which sleep in Jesus will God bring with him. Wherefore comfort one another with these words.

Or else this.

1 Corinthians 15. 50, 53-58.

NOW this I say, brethren, that flesh and blood cannot inherit the kingdom of God; neither doth corruption inherit incorruption. For this corruptible must put on incorruption, and this mortal must put on immortality. So when this corruptible shall have put on incorruption, and this mortal shall have put on immortality, then shall be brought to pass the saying that is written, Death is swallowed up in victory. O death, where is thy sting? O grave, where is thy victory? The sting of death is sin; and the strength of sin is the law. But thanks be to God, which giveth us the victory through our Lord Jesus Christ. Therefore, my beloved brethren, be ye steadfast, unmoveable, always abounding in the work of the Lord, forasmuch as ye know that your labour is not in vain in the Lord.

¶ *Then shall a part of the Gospel of St. John be read.*

St. John 6. 37-40.

ALL that the Father giveth me shall come to me; and him that cometh to me I will in no wise cast out. For I came down from heaven, not to do mine own will, but the will of him that sent me. And this is the Father's will which hath sent me, that of all which he hath given me I should lose nothing, but should raise it up again at the last day. And this is the will of him that sent me, that every one which seeth the Son, and believeth on him, may have everlasting life: and I will raise him up at the last day.

Or this.

St. John 11. 21-26.

THEN said Martha unto Jesus, Lord, if thou hadst been here, my brother had not died. But I know, that even now, whatsoever thou wilt ask of God, God will give it thee. Jesus saith unto her, Thy brother shall rise again. Martha saith unto him, I know that he shall rise again in the resurrection at the last day. Jesus said unto her, I am the resurrection, and the life: he that believeth in me, though he were dead, yet shall he live: and whosoever liveth and believeth in me shall never die.

Or this.

St. John 14. 1-6, 18, 19, 27.

LET not your heart be troubled: ye believe in God, believe also in me. In my Father's house are many mansions: if it were not so, I would have told you. I go to prepare a place for you. And if I go and prepare a place for you, I will come again, and receive you unto myself; that where I am, there ye may be also. And whither I go ye know, and the way ye know. Thomas saith unto him, Lord, we know not whither thou goest; and how can we know the way? Jesus saith unto him, I am the way, the truth, and the life: no man cometh unto the Father, but by me.

I will not leave you comfortless: I will come to you. Yet a little while, and the world seeth me no more; but ye see me: because I live, ye shall live also.

Peace I leave with you, my peace I give unto you: not as the world giveth, give I unto you. Let not your heart be troubled, neither let it be afraid.

THE FELLOWSHIP OF PRAYER

¶ *Then shall follow Thanksgiving and Intercession, the Minister using, if he will, the Prayers set down here.*

Minister. The Lord be with you;

People. And with thy spirit.

Minister. Lift up your hearts;

People. We lift them up unto the Lord.

Minister. Let us give thanks unto our Lord God;

People. It is meet and right so to do.

And the Minister shall continue as followeth.

IT is truly meet, right, and our bounden duty that we should, at all times, and in all places, give thanks unto thee, O Holy Lord, Father Almighty, Everlasting God: But chiefly are we bound to praise thee for him who taketh away the sin of the world, and hath brought life and immortality to light. Therefore with angels and archangels, and with all the company of heaven, we laud and magnify thy glorious name; evermore praising thee, and saying,

HOLY, holy, holy, Lord God of hosts, Heaven and earth are full of thy glory. Glory be to thee, O Lord most high.

ALL glory and thanksgiving be to thee, Almighty God, our heavenly Father, for that thou of thy tender mercy didst give thine only Son Jesus Christ to take our nature upon him, and to suffer death upon the Cross for our redemption. We bless thee for that victory over death and the grave which he hath obtained for us and for all who rest in him; and we pray thee to keep us in everlasting fellowship with all that wait for thee on earth, and with all that are around thee in heaven; in union with him who hath loved us with an everlasting love, and whose life is one with ours, even Jesus Christ our Lord. *Amen.*

ALMIGHTY and merciful God, the consolation of the sorrowful and the support of the weary: Look down in tender love and pity, we beseech thee, upon thy servants whose joy is turned into mourning; so that, while they mourn, they may not murmur, nor faint, but, remembering all thy mercies, thy promises and thy love in Christ, may yield themselves into thy hands, to be taught and disciplined by thee. Fill their desolate hearts with thy love, that they may cleave more closely to thee, who bringest life out of death, and who canst turn their grief into eternal joy; through Jesus Christ our Lord. *Amen.*

O LORD, the God of mercy, unto whom all live: We remember before thee those whom we love but see no longer, unto whom thou givest a place of refreshment, blessed rest, and perfect release from all sin and sorrow, where the light of thy presence shineth for evermore. Grant that we may be united with them in the bliss of thine eternal glory; through Jesus Christ our Lord. *Amen.*

ALMIGHTY God, our heavenly Father, who, in thy perfect wisdom and mercy, hast ended for thy servant departed the voyage of this troublous life; Grant, we beseech thee, that we who are still to continue our course amidst earthly dangers, temptations, and troubles may evermore be protected by thy mercy, and finally come to the haven of eternal salvation; through Jesus Christ our Lord. *Amen.*

OUR Father, who art in heaven, Hallowed be thy name; Thy kingdom come; Thy will be done; In earth as it is in heaven. Give us this day our daily bread. And forgive us our trespasses, As we forgive them that trespass against us. And lead us not into temptation; But deliver us from evil: For thine is the kingdom, The power, and the glory, For ever and ever. Amen.

¶ *Then may a Hymn be sung.*

¶ *Then shall follow the Blessing.*

NOW the God of peace, that brought again from the dead our Lord Jesus, that great Shepherd of the sheep, through the blood of the everlasting covenant, make you perfect in every good work to do his will, working in you that which is well-pleasing in his sight, through Jesus Christ; to whom be glory for ever and ever. *Amen.*

¶ *Other Prayers may be added before the Lord's Prayer.*

¶ *If it be thought expedient to speak some words of comfort and hope, shewing the love of God in the redemption of man by Christ Jesus, how spacious that love is, how tender, how sure, this may be done after the Gospel, or after the Lord's Prayer.*

III

THE BURIAL

¶ *When they come to the grave, while the body is made ready to be laid into the earth, the Minister shall say,*

MAN that is born of a woman is of few days, and full of trouble. He cometh forth like a flower, and is cut down: he fleeth also as a shadow, and continueth not.

Job 14. 1, 2.

IN the midst of life we are in death: of whom may we seek for succour but of thee, O Lord, who for our sins art justly displeased?

Yet, O Lord God most holy, O Lord most mighty, O holy and most merciful Saviour, deliver us not into the bitter pains of eternal death.

Thou knowest, Lord, the secrets of our hearts; shut not thy merciful ears to our prayer; but spare us, Lord most holy, O God most mighty, O holy and merciful Saviour, thou most worthy Judge eternal, suffer us not at our last hour for any pains of death to fall from thee.

Or else he shall say,

Psalm 103. 13-17.

LIKE as a father pitieth his children, so the Lord pitieth them that fear him.

For he knoweth our frame; he remembereth that we are dust.

As for man, his days are as grass: as a flower of the field, so he flourisheth.

For the wind passeth over it, and it is gone: and the place thereof shall know it no more.

But the mercy of the Lord is from everlasting to everlasting upon them that fear him, and his righteousness unto children's children.

Or else,

I AM the resurrection and the life, saith the Lord: he that believeth in me, though he were dead, yet shall he live; and whosoever liveth and believeth in me shall never die. *St. John* 11. 25, 26.

Fear not; I am the first and the last: I am he that liveth and was dead; and behold, I am alive for evermore, and I have the keys of hell and of death. *Revelation* 1. 17, 18.

They shall hunger no more, neither thirst any more; neither shall the sun light on them, nor any heat. For the Lamb which is in the midst of the throne shall feed them, and shall lead them unto living fountains of waters; and God shall wipe away all tears from their eyes. *Revelation* 7. 16, 17.

O death, where is thy sting? O grave, where is thy victory? Thanks be to God, which giveth us the victory through our Lord Jesus Christ. Therefore, my beloved brethren, be ye steadfast, unmoveable, always abounding in the work of the Lord, forasmuch as ye know that your labour is not in vain in the Lord. *1 Corinthians* 15. 55, 57, 58.

¶ *Then, while earth shall be cast upon the body by some standing by, the Minister shall say,*

FORASMUCH as it hath pleased Almighty God to take unto himself the soul of our *brother* (*or* this child) here departed, we therefore commit *his* body to the ground; earth to earth, ashes to ashes, dust to dust; in sure and certain hope of the resurrection to eternal life through our Lord Jesus Christ; who shall change the body of our low estate that it may be like unto his glorious body, according to the mighty working, whereby he is able to subdue all things to himself.

¶ *Then shall be said,*

I HEARD a voice from heaven, saying unto me, Write, From henceforth blessed are the dead which die in the Lord: Even so saith the Spirit: for they rest from their labours.

At the Burial of a Child.

THEY shall hunger no more, neither thirst any more; neither shall the sun light on them, nor any heat. For the Lamb which is in the midst of the throne shall feed them, and shall lead them unto living fountains of waters; and God shall wipe away all tears from their eyes.

THE PRAYERS

¶ *Then may this Litany be said, followed by the Lord's Prayer.*

Minister. Lord, have mercy upon us.
People. Christ, have mercy upon us.
Minister. Lord, have mercy upon us.

OUR Father, who art in heaven; Hallowed be thy name; Thy kingdom come; Thy will be done; In earth as it is in heaven. Give us this day our daily bread. And forgive us our trespasses, As we forgive them that trespass against us. And lead us not into temptation; But deliver us from evil. Amen.

¶ *Then shall follow these Prayers, the Minister first saying,*

Let us pray.

ALMIGHTY God, with whom do live the spirits of them that depart hence in the Lord, and with whom the souls of the faithful, after they are delivered from the burden of the flesh, are in joy and felicity: We beseech thee to hasten thy kingdom; that we, with all those that are departed in the true faith of thy holy name, may have our perfect consummation and bliss, both in body and soul, in thy eternal and everlasting glory; through Jesus Christ our Lord. *Amen.*

O MERCIFUL God, the Father of our Lord Jesus Christ, who is the resurrection and the life; in whom whosoever believeth shall live, though he die; and whosoever liveth and believeth in him shall not die eternally: We beseech thee, O Father, to raise us from the death of sin unto the life of righteousness; that, when we shall depart this life, we may rest in him; and that, at the last day, we may be found acceptable in thy sight; and receive that blessing, which thy well-beloved Son shall then pronounce on all that love and fear thee, saying, Come, ye blessed children of my Father, receive the kingdom prepared for you from the beginning of the world. Grant this, we beseech thee, O merciful Father, through Jesus Christ, our Mediator and Redeemer. *Amen.*

¶ *Then shall be said,*

THE grace of our Lord Jesus Christ, and the love of God, and the communion of the Holy Spirit, be with us all evermore. *Amen.*

¶ *When this Order is used at the cremation of the body, in place of the words,* commit *his* body to the ground, earth to earth, ashes to ashes, dust to dust, *shall be said the words,* commit *his body* to be consumed by fire.

¶ *When this Order is used at the burial of the ashes after cremation, in place of the words,* commit *his* body to the ground, earth to earth, ashes to ashes, dust to dust, *shall be said the words,* commit *his* ashes to the ground, earth to earth, dust to dust, *or* commit *his* ashes to their resting-place.

¶ *When this Order is used at the burial of the dead at sea, in place of the words,* We therefore commit *his* body to the ground, earth to earth, ashes to ashes, dust to dust, *shall be said,* We therefore commit *his* body to the deep, looking for the day of resurrection, when the sea shall give up her dead, and the life of the world to come, through our Lord Jesus Christ; who shall change the body of our low estate that it may be like unto his glorious body, according to the mighty working, whereby he is able to subdue all things to himself.

A PRAYER

Which may be used in specially distressing circumstances.

O GOD of infinite compassion, who art the comforter of thy children: Look down in thy tender love and pity, we beseech thee, upon thy stricken servants, unto whom this trial has come. In the stillness of our hearts we entreat for them thy sustaining grace. Be thou their stay, their strength, and their shield, that they may be delivered from all bitterness, despair, and doubt, trusting in thee to lighten their darkness, and to bring them out of their distress; through Jesus Christ our Lord. *Amen.*

AN ORDER FOR

THE RECEPTION OF CANDIDATES

FOR THE HOLY MINISTRY

¶ *When the time is come for the Reception of Candidates for the Holy Ministry, a Minister appointed by the Presbytery shall call by their names all them that are to be received, and shall present them to the Presbytery, saying,*

FATHERS and Brethren, I present unto you *these persons* to be received as *Candidates* for the Holy Ministry. We have enquired concerning *them,* and also examined *them,* and think *them* worthy to be so received.

¶ *Then shall the Presiding Minister address the Candidates, saying,*

DEARLY beloved sons, you come, for the love of God and with pure intention, to offer *yourselves* for this sacred office, and to take upon *yourselves* the preparation for the same which the Church requires.

God by his Holy Spirit calls men to serve him in the different vocations of life according to the gifts which he bestows upon them; but to some he grants this grace that they should be Ministers of his Word and Sacraments, and shepherds of his flock.

Consider well what you are undertaking; to how weighty an office and charge you aspire, and what a burden will be laid on your shoulders; but consider also, how high is the privilege, how great the joy, and how sure the grace of God.

And now that this Presbytery may understand your mind and will in this thing, we ask of you,

DO you believe in one God, Father, Son, and Holy Spirit; and do you confess anew the Lord Jesus Christ as your Saviour and Lord?

Answer. I do.

DO you trust that you are inwardly moved by the Holy Spirit to present *yourselves* to God, to serve in the Holy Ministry, for the promoting of his glory and the edifying of his people?

Answer. I do.

DO you, therefore, offer *yourselves* willingly for this sacred Office?

Answer. I do.

WILL you give all diligence to frame and fashion your own *lives* according to the teaching and example of Christ?

Answer. I will.

WILL you dutifully submit *yourselves* in the Lord to the authority of this Presbytery?

Answer. I will.

¶ *Then shall the Presiding Minister address the Presbytery, saying,*

LET us, brethren beloved, pray to God for his *servants* here present, who *do* now give *themselves* to the Ministry of the Gospel, that he would send upon *them* his Holy Spirit, to increase in *them* his strength, and enlighten *them* with his everlasting grace.

Here shall silence be kept for a space; after which the Presiding Minister shall pray in this wise.

O GOD, Father eternal, who hast given thy everglorious Son Jesus Christ to be head over all things to thy Church: Mercifully look upon *these* thy *servants* whom we present before thee. Accept *their* vows, we beseech thee; and answer *them* in the abundance of thy grace. Bestow upon *them* thy Holy Spirit, that *they* may understand thy gracious will, and may prove *their* fitness to serve thee in the Ministry of thy Word. Strengthen *their* faith; enlighten *their* minds; confirm *their* courage; deepen *their* joy; and guide *them* and thy Church, if that be thy will, into the full assurance that thou hast called *them* to the Ministry of thy Gospel; through Jesus Christ our Lord. *Amen.*

¶ *Then the Presiding Minister, taking the Candidates severally by the hand, shall say to each,*

IN the name of the Lord Jesus Christ, we receive you as a Candidate for the Ministry of the Word and Sacraments.

May God grant you grace for this work. *Amen.*

¶ *Then shall the Presiding Minister give this Blessing.*

THE peace of God, which passeth all understanding, keep your hearts and minds in the knowledge and love of God, and of his Son Jesus Christ our Lord: and the blessing of God Almighty, Father, Son, and Holy Spirit, be amongst you and remain with you always. *Amen.*

AN ORDER FOR

THE LICENSING OF CANDIDATES

FOR THE HOLY MINISTRY

¶ *When the Presbytery examines a Candidate for the Ministry, and, being satisfied with his character and his proficiency in learning, recommends him to the Conference for Ordination, it does thereby affirm that, in its judgement, he is qualified to preach the Gospel; this fact may be explicitly stated in the resolution recommending the Candidate, and a copy of the resolution may be given him. No further action on the part of the Presbytery is necessary; but if a rite or ceremony be desired, the following Order may be used.*

¶ *They that are to be licensed shall be presented to the Presiding Minister and to the Presbytery.*

¶ *Then shall the Presiding Minister say to the Candidates.*

BELOVED in the Lord, God has given commandment unto his Church, not only to pray for the increase of the Ministry, but also to prove those who seek the sacred Office, that no man be ordained suddenly, but that men of pure heart and right conduct, able to speak to edification, be found for his holy service. This Presbytery, therefore, having enquired concerning you, and also examined you, and having found you to be of good report, of sound faith, and of sufficient learning, does now commend you to the Conference as qualified to preach the Gospel of the grace of God. And we follow you with our prayers.

¶ *Then shall the Presiding Minister say,*

Let us pray.

ALMIGHTY God, who hast given unto thy Son Jesus Christ to be head over all things to thy Church: We beseech thee to bestow upon *these* thy *servants* the grace of thy Holy Spirit, that *they* may be endued with power to preach thy Gospel, and may prove *their* fitness to serve thee in the Ministry of the Word. Replenish *them* with the truth of thy doctrine, and adorn *them* with innocency of life, that *they* may faithfully serve thee both by word and example. Give *them* grace to preach the unsearchable riches of Christ, to instruct with meekness those that oppose themselves to the truth, and to gather into the fold of Christ many that are wandering in the ways of error and sin. Grant that, going forth and labouring in dependence upon thee, they may have abundant fruit of *their* labours, and obtain the reward of faithful servants (*or* a faithful servant) in thy heavenly kingdom; through Jesus Christ our Lord. *Amen.*

OUR Father, who art in heaven, Hallowed be thy name; Thy kingdom come; Thy will be done; In earth as it is in heaven. Give us this day our daily bread. And forgive us our trespasses, As we forgive them that trespass against us. And lead us not into temptation; But deliver us from evil: For thine is the kingdom, The power, and the glory, For ever and ever. Amen.

¶ *And he may bless them, saying,*

THE Word of the Lord be nigh you, even in your mouth, and in your heart.

The blessing of God Almighty, the Father, the Son, and the Holy Spirit, be with you. *Amen.*

¶ *It is to be noted that this Licensing of a Candidate to preach is no part of Ordination to the Ministry.*

THE ORDER FOR

THE ORDINATION OF MINISTERS

¶ *When the time appointed for Ordination is come, a Psalm or Hymn shall be sung.*

¶ *Then shall a Minister appointed thereto present all them that are to be ordained to the Presiding Minister and the other Ministers in the manner following, first saying,*

Let all those who are to be ordained come forward.

And when they stand in their place he shall say,

REVEREND President, Fathers, and Brethren, I present unto you these persons to be admitted Ministers of the Word and Sacraments.

Here he shall read their names.

We have inquired of them, and also examined them, and think them to be fit and worthy to exercise this Ministry.

¶ *Then the Presiding Minister shall say to the People,*

BRETHREN, these are they whom we purpose, God willing, this day to ordain to the holy Ministry. For after due examination, we find that they are lawfully called to this Function and Office, and that they are persons meet for the same. But if there be any of you who knoweth anything against any of them, for which he ought not to be received into this holy Ministry, let him come forth in the name of God, and show what the impediment is.

¶ *After a pause, the Presiding Minister shall move the people to pray, saying,*

I COMMEND these that have been found meet to be ordained, to the prayers of the Congregation.

Here shall silence be kept for a space, that prayer may be made for them that are to be ordained.

¶ *Then shall the Presiding Minister proceed in the service for the Communion, in which the Prayer for Grace, Epistle, and Gospel shall be as followeth.*

The Prayer for Grace.

ALMIGHTY God, giver of all good things, who by thy Holy Spirit hast appointed the Ministry of the Word and Sacraments: Mercifully behold these thy servants now called to this holy Office, and replenish them so with the truth of thy doctrine, and adorn them with innocency of life, that, both by word and good example, they may faithfully serve thee in this Office, to the glory of thy name, and the edification of thy Church; through the merits of our Saviour Jesus Christ, who liveth and reigneth with thee and the Holy Spirit, world without end. *Amen.*

The Epistle. Ephesians 4. 4-8, 11-13.

THERE is one body, and one Spirit, even as ye are called in one hope of your calling; one Lord, one faith, one baptism, one

God and Father of all, who is above all, and through all, and in you all. But unto every one of us is given grace, according to the measure of the gift of Christ. Wherefore he saith, when he ascended up on high, he led captivity captive, and gave gifts unto men. And he gave some apostles, and some prophets, and some evangelists, and some pastors and teachers; for the perfecting of the saints, for the work of the ministry, for the edifying of the body of Christ; till we all come in the unity of the faith, and of the knowledge of the Son of God, unto a perfect man, unto the measure of the stature of the fullness of Christ.

The Gospel. St. John 21. 15-17.

JESUS saith to Simon Peter, Simon, son of Jonas, lovest thou me more than these? He saith unto him, Yea, Lord, thou knowest that I love thee. He saith unto him, Feed my lambs. He saith to him again the second time, Simon, son of Jonas, lovest thou me? He saith unto him, Yea, Lord, thou knowest that I love thee. He saith unto him, Feed my sheep. He saith unto him the third time, Simon, son of Jonas, lovest thou me? Peter was grieved because he said unto him the third time, Lovest thou me? And he said unto him, Lord, thou knowest all things;

thou knowest that I love thee. Jesus saith unto him, Feed my sheep.

Or this.

St. John 10. 1-11.

VERILY, verily, I say unto you, He that entereth not by the door into the sheepfold, but climbeth up some other way, the same is a thief and a robber. But he that entereth in by the door is the shepherd of the sheep. To him the porter openeth; and the sheep hear his voice: and he calleth his own sheep by name, and leadeth them out. And when he putteth forth his own sheep, he goeth before them, and the sheep follow him: for they know his voice. And a stranger will they not follow, but will flee from him: for they know not the voice of strangers. This parable spake Jesus unto them: but they understood not what things they were which he spake unto them. Then said Jesus unto them again, Verily, verily, I say unto you, I am the door of the sheep. All that ever came before me are thieves and robbers: but the sheep did not hear them. I am the door: by me if any man enter in, he shall be saved, and shall go in and out, and find pasture. The thief cometh not, but for to steal, and to kill, and to destroy: I am come that they might have life, and that they might have it more abundantly. I am the good shepherd: the good shepherd giveth his life for the sheep.

Or this.

St. Matthew 28. 18-20.

AND Jesus came and spake unto them, saying, All power is given unto me in heaven and in earth. Go ye therefore, and teach all nations, baptizing them in the name of the Father, and of the Son, and of the Holy Ghost: teaching them to observe all things whatsoever I have commanded you: and, lo, I am with you alway, even unto the end of the world.

¶ *Then shall follow a Sermon, declaring the Duty and Office of such as come to be admitted Ministers of the Word and Sacraments; how necessary that Order is in the Church of Christ, and also how the People ought to esteem them in their Office.*

¶ *Then shall follow a Prayer for the whole state of Christ's Church.*

¶ *After this, the Presiding Minister shall say unto them that are to be ordained,*

YOU have heard, Brethren, as well in your private examination, as in the exhortation which was now made to you, and in the holy Lessons taken out of the Gospel, and the writings of the Apostles, of what dignity, and of how great importance this Office is, whereunto you are called. And now again we exhort you, in the name of our Lord Jesus Christ, that you have in remembrance, into how high a dignity, and to how weighty an office and charge you are called: that is to say, to be Messengers, Watchmen, and Stewards of the Lord; to teach, and to admonish, to feed and provide for the Lord's family; to seek for Christ's sheep that are dispersed abroad, and for his children who are in the midst of this evil world, that they may be saved through Christ for ever.

Have always, therefore, in remembrance how great a treasure is committed to your charge. For the Church and Congregation whom you must serve is the Spouse and the Body of Christ. And if it shall happen that his Church, or any Member thereof, do take any hurt or hindrance by reason of your negligence, you know the greatness of the fault. See, therefore, that you never cease your labour, your care and diligence, until you have done all that lieth in you to bring such as are committed to your charge to the faith and knowledge of God, and to perfectness of life in Christ.

We have good hope that you have well weighed and pondered these things with yourselves long before this time; and that you have clearly determined, by God's grace, to give yourselves wholly to this Office whereunto it has pleased God to call you; so that, as much as lieth in you, you will apply yourselves to this one thing, and draw all your cares and studies this way; and that you will continually pray to God for the fullness of his grace, that by daily reading and weighing of the Scriptures, you may grow riper and stronger in your Ministry; and that you will strive to fashion the lives of you and yours after the rule and teaching of Christ, that you may be wholesome and godly examples and patterns for the people to follow.

And now that this Congregation of Christ here assembled may also understand your mind and will in these things, and that this your promise may the more move you to do your duties, you shall answer plainly to these things which we, in the name of God, and of his Church, shall ask of you touching the same.

DO you believe yourself to be a child of God, through faith in our Lord Jesus Christ?

Answer. I do so believe.

The Presiding Minister.

DO you believe yourself to be called of God to the Office of the Christian Ministry, and your chief motives to be zeal for the glory of God, love for the Lord Jesus Christ, and desire for the salvation of men?

Answer. I do so believe.

The Presiding Minister

ARE you persuaded that the holy Scriptures contain sufficiently all doctrines required for eternal salvation in our Lord Jesus Christ?

and are you resolved out of the said Scriptures to instruct the people committed to your charge, and to teach nothing which is not agreeable thereto?

Answer. I am so persuaded, and am so resolved, by God's grace.

¶ *Then shall the Presiding Minister say,*

ALMIGHTY God, who hath given you the will to do all these things: Grant also unto you strength and power to perform the same; that he may accomplish his work which he hath begun in you; through Jesus Christ our Lord. *Amen.*

¶ *After this, the Presiding Minister shall say to the People,*

LET us pray, dear brethren, that God in his loving kindness may bestow a plentiful grace upon these his servants; that what things they now undertake through his gracious call, they may, by his help, be enabled to fulfil.

¶ *Then shall the Congregation make their humble supplications to God; for the which Prayers silence shall be kept for a space.*

¶ *After which shall be sung or said* Veni Creator Spiritus (*the persons to be ordained all kneeling*).

COME, Holy Ghost, our souls inspire,
And lighten with celestial fire;
Thou the anointing Spirit art,
Who dost thy sevenfold gifts impart.

Thy blessed unction from above
Is comfort, life, and fire of love.
Enable with perpetual light
The dullness of our blinded sight;

Anoint and cheer our soilèd face
With the abundance of thy grace;
Keep far our foes; give peace at home:
Where thou art Guide no ill can come.

Teach us to know the Father, Son,
And thee of both to be but One.
That through the ages all along
This may be our endless song:

Praise to thy eternal merit,
Father, Son, and Holy Spirit.

¶ *That done, the Presiding Minister shall pray in this wise, and say,*

Lift up your hearts.

Answer. We lift them up unto the Lord.

Minister. Let us give thanks unto our Lord God.

Answer. It is meet and right so to do.

Then shall the Presiding Minister continue,

IT is very meet, right, and our bounden duty, that we should at all times, and in all places, give thanks unto thee, O Holy Lord, Father Almighty, Everlasting God: Who, of thine infinite love and goodness towards us, hast given to us thy only and most dearly beloved Son Jesus Christ, to be our Redeemer, and the Author of everlasting life; who, after he had made perfect our redemption by his death, and was ascended into heaven, sent abroad into the world his Apostles, Prophets, Evangelists, Pastors and Teachers, by whose labour and ministry he gathered together a great flock in all the parts of the world, to set forth the eternal praise of thy holy name: For these so great benefits of thy eternal goodness, and for that thou hast vouchsafed to call these thy servants here present to the same Office and Ministry appointed for the salvation of mankind, we render unto thee most hearty thanks, we praise and worship thy holy name; through Jesus Christ our Lord. *Amen.*

O GOD, the Source of all authority and of all holiness, of whom are true consecration and the fullness of blessing: Send down, we pray thee, thy Holy Spirit upon these thy servants, whom we, in thy name, do now Ordain and Set apart to be Ministers in thy Church, committing unto them authority to minister thy Word and Sacraments. Grant unto them such fullness of thy grace that they may be faithful and wise stewards whom thou settest over thy household to give to thy family their portion in due season. May constant faith, pure love, true peace abound in them. Grant them, O

Lord, the ministry of reconciliation, in word and in deed, and in thy power. Bestow on them the keys of the kingdom of heaven, that they may meetly use the power thou givest them to save and not to destroy. May they be in care unwearying, in spirit fervent, hating pride; lovers of humility and truth, yielding neither to flattery nor menace. Be thou unto them authority, power, and steadfastness. Multiply upon them thy blessing and thy grace that in all things they may be found faithful, and at last be received, by thy mercy, into glory and immortality in thine eternal kingdom; through our Lord Jesus Christ, who liveth and reigneth with thee and the Holy Ghost, ever one God, world without end. *Amen.*

¶ *When this Prayer is done, the Presiding Minister, with two or more of the Ministers present, shall lay their hands upon the head of every one that receiveth Ordination, the Receivers humbly kneeling upon their knees, and the Presiding Minister saying,*

THE Lord pour upon thee the Holy Spirit for the Office and Work of a Minister in the Church of God, now committed unto thee by the authority of the Church through the Imposition of our hands. And be thou a faithful Dispenser of the Word of God, and of his holy Sacraments; In the name of the Father, and of the Son, and of the Holy Spirit. Amen.

¶ *Then the Presiding Minister shall deliver to every one of them, kneeling, the Bible into his hand, saying,*

TAKE thou Authority to preach the Word of God, and to minister the holy Sacraments in the Congregation.

¶ *When this is done, the Presiding Minister shall go on in the celebration of the Holy Communion.*

¶ *After the Thanksgiving for Communion and the Prayer for grace to persevere, the Presiding Minister shall give this or the like solemn Charge to them that have been ordained.*

DEARLY beloved brethren, consider attentively the Order you have taken, and the burden laid on your shoulders. Endeavour to lead a holy and godly life, and to please Almighty God that you may obtain his grace, which may he of his mercy be pleased to grant you; and do you also pray to Almighty God for us.

¶ *Then shall this Prayer be said.*

MOST merciful Father, we beseech thee to send down upon these thy servants thy heavenly blessing; and so endue them with thy Holy Spirit, that they, preaching thy Word, may not only be earnest to reprove, beseech, and rebuke, with all patience and doctrine; but also may be to such as believe wholesome examples, in word, in conversation, in love, in faith, in charity, and in purity;

that, faithfully fulfilling their course, at the latter day they may receive the crown of righteousness laid up by the Lord the righteous Judge; who liveth and reigneth one God with the Father and the Holy Ghost, world without end. *Amen.*

¶ *Here may be sung a Psalm or Hymn.*

¶ *Then shall follow the Benediction.*

¶ *The Charge may be given to the newly-ordained immediately after the delivery of the Bible.*

¶ *It is an ancient and laudable custom that Ordination should take place in connection with the highest and most solemn act of common worship, namely, the Lord's Supper. But if there be no Communion, the Order here set forth shall be followed to the delivery of the Bible; after which shall be said Prayers of Thanksgiving and Intercession, with special Supplication for the newly-ordained; a Psalm or Hymn shall be sung, and the Blessing given.*

AN ORDER FOR ADMITTING A MINISTER FROM ANOTHER CHURCH

¶ *When a Minister from another Church is to be admitted, one appointed thereto shall present him to the Conference, saying,*

REVEREND President, Fathers and Brethren, I present to you N. N., a minister of the Church of God, that he may receive authority to exercise his ministry in The United Church of Canada.

¶ *Then shall the Presiding Minister say,*

MY brother, do you accept the doctrine and polity of The United Church of Canada? and do you promise to submit yourself to lawful authority within the same?

Answer. I do.

¶ *Then shall he be admitted with these words.*

IN the name of the Lord Jesus Christ, the King and Head of the Church, we admit you to take part with us in the Ministry of the Word and Sacraments within The United Church of Canada.

And the Presiding Minister may add this Blessing.

THE Lord bless thee, and keep thee: the Lord make his face to shine upon thee, and be gracious unto thee: the Lord lift up his countenance upon thee, and give thee peace. *Amen.*

¶ *Then may follow a Prayer for the newly-admitted Minister.*

AN ORDER FOR

THE INDUCTION OF A MINISTER

¶ *On the day appointed, there shall be Divine Service, with these Lessons,* 1 St. Peter 5: 1-4; St. John 21: 15-17, *and a Sermon on the Office and Duty of Ministers of Christ and how the People ought to receive them for their work's sake.*

¶ *The Sermon being ended, the Presiding Minister shall say to the People,*

BELOVED in the Lord, In the name of God, and in the presence of this Congregation, we purpose now to institute and induct to the pastoral charge of this Church, our brother in Christ, N. N., here present.

¶ *The Minister-elect shall then be presented before the Presbytery and the People, and the Presiding Minister shall say to the People,*

BELOVED in the Lord, do you receive this our brother as your Minister in the Lord, promising to labour with him in faith and prayer for the honour of Christ, and the comfort of his Church?

Then shall the People, or else one or more by them appointed thereto make answer and say,

We do so receive him.

¶ *Then shall the Presiding Minister say to the Minister-elect,*

MY brother, seeing that the grace of God and the choice of the Church have called you to the cure of souls in this place, and that this Congregation of Christ may understand your mind and will in this thing, we ask of you, in sincere charity, whether you be willing to take upon you so sacred and grave a charge.

Answer. I am willing, the Lord being my helper.

WILL you then give your faithful diligence always so to minister to this People the Doctrine and Sacraments and Discipline of Christ, as the Lord hath commanded, and as the Church hath received the same?

Answer. I will do so, by the help of the Lord.

WILL you maintain and set forward, as much as lieth in you, quietness, peace, and love among all Christian people, and especially among them that are committed to your charge?

Answer. I will do so, the Lord being my helper.

WILL you, as a man compassed with infirmities, receive in charity the admonition of your brethren, and be subject to the discipline of the Church, as the rest of your brethren?

Answer. I do so promise, the Lord being my helper.

Then shall the Presiding Minister say,

ALMIGHTY God, who hath given you the will to do all these things: Grant also unto you strength and power to perform the same; that he may accomplish his work which he hath begun in you; through Jesus Christ our Lord. *Amen.*

¶ *Then shall the Presiding Minister say to the Minister-elect,*

IN the name of the Lord Jesus Christ, the King and Head of the Church, and by the authority of this Presbytery, I Institute and Induct you to the Pastoral Charge of this Church. Receive this Cure of Souls which is both ours and yours.

Adding also,

THE Lord preserve thy going out and thy coming in from this time forth for evermore. *Amen.*

¶ *Then shall the Presiding Minister say to the People,*

YOU have heard, dear brethren, the duty and profession of this our brother, appointed to this Charge; as also the duty which God requires of you; and because none of us is able to perform anything without the grace of God, let us pray that he may sanctify this ministry begun to his glory and the comfort of his Church.

Then the Presiding Minister shall say,

O Lord, save thy servant;

People. Who putteth his trust in thee.

Minister. Send him help from thy holy place;

People. And evermore defend him.

Then shall silence be kept for a space so that prayer may be made to God.

¶ *After which may be sung or said* Veni Creator Spiritus (*The Hymnary, No.* 143).

¶ *That done, the Presiding Minister shall pray in this wise.*

BLESS, O Lord, we beseech thee, thy servant to whom the care of the souls of thy people in this Church and Congregation is now committed. Pour out thy Holy Spirit upon him that he may fulfil his sacred duties with all faithfulness, diligence, and courage. Give to him the spirit of power, and of love, and of a sound mind. Make his ministry to be the means of awakening the careless, strengthening the faithful, comforting the afflicted, building up thy Church, and converting sinners unto thee. Guard him against the snares of temptation, that he may be kept pure in heart, fervent in spirit, valiant against evil. And grant that at last he may receive the crown of life which thou hast promised to thy faithful servants; through Jesus Christ our Lord. *Amen.*

O LORD God, the Sanctifier of the faithful: Visit, we pray thee, this Congregation with thy love and favour; prepare their hearts to receive thy Word; enlighten their minds more and more with the light of the everlasting Gospel; increase in them true religion; nourish them with all goodness; and of thy great mercy keep them in the unity of the spirit and in the bonds of love; through Jesus Christ our Lord. *Amen.*

OUR Father, who art in heaven, Hallowed be thy name; Thy kingdom come; Thy will be done; In earth as it is in heaven. Give us this day our daily bread. And forgive us our trespasses, As we forgive them that trespass against us. And lead us not into temptation; But deliver us from evil: For thine is the kingdom, The power, and the glory, For ever and ever. Amen.

¶ *If it be desirable to add anything to the instruction contained in the Sermon, a brief Charge to Minister and People may here be given.*

¶ *The Minister having been inducted shall then be brought (the People standing) to the place of his ministry in the Church.*

¶ *Then the Presiding Minister shall say,*

Let us pray.

O FATHER, the Shepherd and Ruler of all the faithful: Give thy grace to thy servant, whom thou hast been pleased to set in this place. Grant that by word and example he may so profit those committed to his charge that together they may attain everlasting life; through Jesus Christ our Lord. *Amen.*

¶ *A Hymn may then be sung.*

¶ *Then the Presiding Minister shall leave him in his place, and the Minister inducted shall give this or the like solemn Benediction, saying,*

THE grace of the Lord Jesus Christ, and the love of God, and the communion of the Holy Spirit, be with you. *Amen.*

AN ORDER FOR THE

INSTALLATION OF A DIRECTOR OF CHRISTIAN EDUCATION, A DEACONESS, OR AN ASSISTANT TO THE MINISTER

¶ *At a fitting time in the Service of Public Worship, the person to be installed shall come forward.*

¶ *Then shall the Minister say to the People,*

DEARLY beloved, I present to you N. who has been called to serve in this congregation.

¶ *Addressing the person who is to be installed the Minister shall say,*

BELOVED in Christ, since you have been chosen to labour among this people in Christian service, and that this congregation may understand your mind and will concerning your labours, I ask of you,

DO you believe in one God, Father, Son, and Holy Spirit; and do you confess anew Jesus Christ as your Saviour and Lord?

Answer. I do.

WILL you, in the strength of the Lord Jesus Christ, walk worthy of your calling, and discharge faithfully the duties of your office?

Answer. I will endeavour to do so, God helping me.

DO you promise, as God shall give you grace, to seek earnestly the peace and welfare of this congregation, to be obedient to those in authority over your work, and in all things to be subject to the government and the discipline of the Church?

Answer. I do so promise, God helping me.

¶ *Then may the person who is to be installed kneel, and the Minister shall pray in this wise,*

ALMIGHTY God, eternal Father, who hast revealed thy love in Jesus Christ our Lord, and called us to be fellow-labourers with him in his Church and kingdom: We commend thy servant here before thee to thy continual love and guidance. Endue *him* with thy grace, that *he* may be filled with the strength and gentleness of Christ. Sustain *him* amidst all trials and difficulties. Give *him* a right judgment in all things; bestow upon *him* the grace of perseverance; and enable *him* by word and deed to manifest the spirit of his Lord.

As *he* enters the homes of the people, grant *him* also an entrance into their hearts, that with wise and loving sympathy *he* may comfort the sick, cheer the aged, raise up the fallen, strengthen such as do stand, bring back those who have wandered and gone astray, and win the hearts of the young to the faith of the Gospel and the service of Christ the Lord. Grant *him* grace so to glorify thee on earth that, when *he* has finished the work which thou givest *him* to do, *he* may receive the crown of glory that fadeth not away; through Jesus Christ our Lord, *Amen.*

¶ *The person who is to be installed may rise and the Minister shall say,*

IN the name of the Lord Jesus Christ, I do now set you apart as ....

THE blessing of God Almighty, Father, Son, and Holy Spirit, rest upon you and abide with you always. *Amen.*

¶ *Then shall the Minister go on in the Service of Public Worship.*

AN ORDER FOR

THE ADMISSION OF MEMBERS OF SESSION

TO THEIR OFFICE

¶ *After the Sermon, bearing on the nature and work of the Office, the Minister shall call by their names them that are to be admitted Members of Session, and they shall stand before him, and he shall then say to them,*

DEAR brethren, the Church, which is the Body of Christ, is composed of many members with diversities of heavenly gifts, and all members one of another, to the increase and edifying of the Body in love; though all members have not the same office. You have been called, by the grace of God and the choice of the people, to the Office of Elder in this Church. You are, therefore, to consider well the sacred Charge which you are now to take upon you. It belongs to this Office to join with the Minister of the Word and Sacraments in the exercise of godly and spiritual government and discipline in the Church of God. And it is your duty severally to assist the Pastor in the oversight of the people, for their comfort and steadfastness in Christ.

Be you then earnest in all goodness, in honesty, and persevering charity, that you may be a profit and a delight to the family of God, which is his Church.

Now that this congregation may understand your mind and will in this thing, we ask of you, in sincere charity, whether you be willing to take upon you so sacred and grave an Office.

Answer. I am willing, the Lord being my helper.

DO you confess Jesus Christ as your Saviour and Lord?

Answer. I do so confess him.

WILL you be diligent to frame and fashion your own lives and the lives of your families according to the teaching of Christ?

Answer. I will do so, the Lord being my helper.

WILL you maintain and set forward as much as in you lieth quietness, peace, and love among all Christian people, and especially among them of this Congregation?

Answer. I will do so, the Lord being my helper.

¶ *The Minister shall then say,*

ALMIGHTY God accept and bless you, and grant you the power and strength to perform all these things to the edifying of his Church and the honour of his name. *Amen.*

¶ *The Elders-elect may then kneel, and the Minister shall call the People to take their part in what is to be done, saying,*

DEARLY beloved brethren, let us pray to God the Father Almighty that he may pour out upon these his servants his heavenly blessing; through Christ our Lord.

Then shall the People make their supplications to God; for which prayers silence shall be kept for a space.

¶ *After which may be sung or said* Veni Creator Spiritus (*The Hymnary, No.* 143).

¶ *Then shall the Minister pray in this wise.*

ALMIGHTY God, our heavenly Father, who of thine infinite goodness hast given thy Son Jesus Christ to be our redeemer and the author of everlasting life, and hast made him to be head over all things to the Church, wherein thou hast appointed Ministers of thy word, and joined with them faithful men to guard and guide thy flock: Send down thy Holy Spirit upon these thy servants whom we, in thy name, set apart to the Work and Office of Government in thy Church. Endue them with heavenly wisdom, that in counsel they may deal wisely as those who have the mind of Christ. May they be pure in heart, earnest in purpose, and lowly in personal claim. Grant them increase in thy truth as it is in Jesus, and fill them with love and tender care for every soul for whom he vouchsafed to die; that through their labours thy Church may be increased and edified;

to the glory of thy Son our blessed Lord Jesus, who with thee and the Holy Spirit liveth and reigneth, ever one God, world without end. *Amen.*

¶ *Then shall the Minister say,*

IN the name of the Lord Jesus Christ, I admit you to the Session of this Church.

THE blessing of God Almighty, Father, Son, and Holy Spirit, rest upon you and abide with you always. *Amen.*

¶ *A Charge may here be given to the newly-admitted Elders and to the People.*

¶ *In this Order the word* Elder, *being in common use, is to be understood as having the same meaning as* Member of Session *in the Basis of Union.*

¶ *In this Order the word* admit, *being free from ambiguity and in common use, is to be understood as having the same meaning as* set apart or ordain *in section* 9 (*a*) *of the Polity in the Basis of Union.*

AN ORDER FOR
THE INSTALLATION OF MEMBERS OF THE COMMITTEE OF STEWARDS
TO THEIR OFFICE

¶ *At a fitting time in the Service of Public Worship the Minister shall call by their names them that are to be installed Members of the Committee of Stewards, and they shall stand before him, and he shall say to them,*

DEAR brethren, you have been called by the grace of God and the choice of the people, to the Office of Steward in this Church. It belongs to this Office to administer the temporal affairs of the congregation and thus to serve the kingdom of God. May you have joy in faithful service, knowing that in dedicating your time and talents to the good of Christ's Church you are workers together with God.

Now that this congregation may understand your mind and will in this thing, we ask you, in sincere charity, whether you be willing to take upon you so important and necessary an Office.

Answer. I am willing, the Lord being my helper.

DO you promise to give diligent service in the temporal affairs of this congregation?

Answer. I do so promise, the Lord being my helper.

WILL you maintain and set forward as much as in you lieth quietness, peace, and love among all Christian people, and especially among them of this congregation?

Answer. I will do so, the Lord being my helper.

¶ *The Stewards elect may then kneel, and the Minister shall pray in this wise.*

O LORD, our God, who art the only founder and keeper of thy Church: We thank thee that thou hast called these thy servants to share in the work of thy kingdom. Grant them sincerity, singleness of mind, and grace to give themselves to this their task and service. Guide them in their work for thy Church. Prosper their counsels and their labours. Reward their fidelity with the knowledge that thou art using them for the accomplishment of thy purpose in Jesus Christ our Lord. *Amen.*

¶ *Then may the Stewards-elect rise and the Minister shall say,*

IN the Name of the Lord Jesus Christ, I install you Members of the Committee of Stewards of this Church.

THE blessing of God Almighty, Father, Son, and Holy Spirit, rest upon you and abide with you always. *Amen.*

¶ *Then shall the Minister go on in the Service of Public Worship.*

AN ORDER FOR
THE INSTALLATION OF TEACHERS
IN A CHURCH SCHOOL

¶ *When the time is come, the names of them that are to be installed shall be read.*

¶ *Then may the Minister, if he will, read a Lesson taken from the Holy Scripture.* Deuteronomy 6. 4-8; *or* 2 Timothy 1. 1-14; *or* 2 Timothy 2. 1-15; *or* St. Luke 2. 41-52.

¶ *Then shall he give to them that are to be installed such instruction as he may think expedient touching their work and duty. And he may ask these questions.*

DO you believe in one God, Father, Son, and Holy Spirit; and do you confess anew Jesus Christ as your Saviour and Lord?

Answer. I do.

WILL you discharge faithfully the duties of your office?

Answer. I will endeavour so to do, God helping me.

¶ *Then shall the Minister say to them,*

IN the name of the Lord Jesus Christ, I admit you Teachers in this School.

THE Lord bless you, and keep you: the Lord make his face to shine upon you, and be gracious unto you: the Lord lift up his countenance upon you, and give you peace. *Amen.*

¶ *Then shall be said one or more of the Prayers, following, with the Lord's Prayer*

ETERNAL and everliving Father, who dost call us into thy service and dost promise grace and strength for the fulfilling of thy will: Look with favour upon these thy servants who now dedicate themselves to their task in this school. Lead them to a deeper knowledge of their Saviour. Enlighten them in the understanding of thy Word. Grant them insight and patience. And help them so to follow their Master that those who are taught by them may be led in the way everlasting; through Jesus Christ our Lord. *Amen.*

O HEAVENLY Father, who long ago didst watch thy Son grow as in stature so in wisdom and in perfect love of thee: Teach by the wondrous tale of Jesus and his Church the children whom thou watchest now; that they may grow into his likeness, loving thee, obedient to thy will, and happy in thy house; through the same Jesus Christ our Lord. *Amen.*

O LORD, without whom our labour is but lost, and with whom thy little ones go forth as the mighty: Be present at all works in thy Church which are undertaken according to thy will (*especially* . . .), and grant to thy labourers a pure intention, patient faith, sufficient success upon earth, and the bliss of serving thee in heaven; through Jesus Christ our Lord. *Amen.*

¶ *The officers of any society in the Church may be installed in the same way; that is, after suitable instruction, the Minister may admit them to their office, and then in prayer entreat the Lord's grace for them.*

AN ORDER FOR

THE SENDING FORTH OF A MISSIONARY

¶ *The Sending forth of a Missionary shall be conjoined with a celebration of the Lord's Supper or with Public Worship.*

¶ *The Service shall proceed to the Lessons from Holy Scripture; then before a Lesson is read he who is to be sent forth shall be presented to the Presiding Minister and the other Ministers.*

¶ *Then shall the Presiding Minister say,*

Let us pray.

HEARKEN, O Lord, to the prayers of thy people, and with thy never-failing protection guard them that do thee service with a devout heart, that, unhindered by any disturbance, we may ever in our ministries render unto thee that service which is perfect freedom; through Jesus Christ our Lord. *Amen.*

¶ *Then shall be read a Lesson taken from the Holy Scripture.* Isaiah 6. 1-8, *or* 52. 7-10, *and* Acts 1. 8.

¶ *Then shall the Presiding Minister say to him who is to be sent forth,*

BELOVED in the Lord, you come, for the love of God, and in sincere devotion, desiring to be sent forth a Missionary of our Lord Jesus Christ, through whom God has revealed himself in his power and grace to all mankind. You know well that to the

Church has been committed the proclamation of his Gospel, and that to chosen servants is granted this grace that they should go and tell abroad the message, and bring to men the gift of Christ crucified and living.

We are persuaded that you have heard this call and have pondered well to what an office and work you devote yourself. And now, as the burden of this mission is laid upon your shoulders, we bid you to remember that the grace of God is sufficient for you in every time of need. We also bid you to have in mind how high is the privilege, and how great the joy of bringing many to the knowledge and fellowship of our Lord and Saviour.

Be assured that, as God gives us grace, we will not cease to uphold you, for the calling is both ours and yours.

And now, that this congregation here present may know your mind and will in this thing, I ask of you,

DO you believe that God has called you to the office and work of a Missionary of his Gospel?

Answer. I do.

WILL you, in the strength of the Lord Jesus Christ, walk worthy of your calling, and discharge faithfully the duties of your office?

Answer. I will endeavour to do so, God helping me.

DO you promise to seek the unity and peace of the Church, and to yield yourself to the authority of those to whom the Church has committed the direction of your work?

Answer. I do so promise, God helping me.

¶ *Then shall the Presiding Minister say,*

ALMIGHTY God bless thee, and be thy helper in these and all other good things. *Amen.*

¶ *Then shall the Presiding Minister say to the People,*

BRETHREN, let us now with one accord make our supplication to Almighty God on behalf of this his servant, that he may grant him grace to fulfil his office and work.

Then shall follow this Prayer, the Candidate kneeling.

ALL glory, praise, and thanksgiving be unto thee, O Lord our God, for that thou didst reveal thy tender love for the children of men in sending thy beloved Son for their redemption, and hast from the beginning raised up chosen servants to tell abroad the message of thy grace.

We give thee thanks for the devotion of this thy servant whom we now, in thy name, send forth to bear the same message.

(*Reference may here be made to the particular kind of work to which he is sent forth.*) Accept his love and devotion; and increase in him, we beseech thee, the gifts of thy Holy Spirit, that he may commend by teaching and example the grace of the Lord Jesus. Give him understanding, sympathy, and patience; guard him in peril of body and of soul; be thou his strength and his joy; cheer him with thy continual presence; and make him glad with the fruits of his labour.

And we beseech thee to help us who send him forth to bear him up continually with prayer and loving thought; through Jesus Christ our Lord. *Amen.*

¶ *Then shall the Presiding Minister say,*

WE dedicate and send you forth a Missionary of Jesus Christ: In the name of the Father, and of the Son, and of the Holy Ghost. *Amen.*

¶ *And he shall deliver unto him the Bible, saying,*

BE diligent to study the things which are written in this Book, that, as much as in you lieth, you may teach the Gospel of the grace of God, and be an example of faith and of holy living.

¶ *Then shall the Presiding Minister proceed in the Service of the Communion or of Public Worship; and first, a Psalm or Hymn may be sung.*

¶ *Then shall a second Lesson be read: St.* Matthew 28. 16-20, *or St.* Mark 16. 9-20; *or St.* Luke 10. 1-20, *or* Ephesians 3.

¶ *Then shall follow the Sermon.*

¶ *Before the Benediction this Prayer shall be said.*

ALMIGHTY God, who art the giver of all spiritual grace, and the author of everlasting life: Look with thy favour upon this thy servant, and grant him grace, that he may know what things he ought to do, and have strength to do them; through Jesus Christ our Lord. *Amen.*

AN ORDER FOR
THE SENDING FORTH OF WOMEN MISSIONARIES
AND FOR
THE SETTING APART OF DEACONESSES

¶ *The Sending forth of Women Missionaries and the Setting apart of Deaconesses shall be conjoined with the celebration of the Lord's Supper or with Public Worship.*

¶ *The Service shall proceed to the Prayer for Grace.*

¶ *Then shall the President of the Conference say,*

Let those who are to be sent forth Missionaries come forward.

¶ *Then shall they be presented to the Conference by one representing a Board or Society to which authority to examine and appoint Missionaries has been given, or by one appointed thereto by the Conference, and in this wise.*

REVEREND President, Fathers and Brethren, I present unto you these women here present to be dedicated and sent forth Missionaries of our Lord Jesus Christ.

Here their names shall be read.

We have inquired of them, and also examined them, and think them fit and worthy to exercise this vocation.

Then shall the Presiding Minister say to the People,

BRETHREN, these are they whom we purpose, God willing, this day to send forth Missionaries. If any of you knoweth any just cause why any of them should not be so sent forth, let him now come forward and declare it.

¶ *After a pause the President of the Conference shall say,*

Let those who are to be set apart Deaconesses come forward.

¶ *Then shall a Minister appointed thereto present them to the Presiding Minister, saying,*

REVEREND President, Fathers and Brethren, I present unto you these women to be admitted Deaconesses.

Here their names shall be read.

We have inquired of them and also examined them, and think them fit and worthy to exercise this ministry.

Then shall the Presiding Minister say to the People,

BRETHREN, these are they whom we purpose, God willing, this day to set apart to be Deaconesses. If any of you knoweth any just cause why any of them should not be so set apart, let him now come forward and declare it.

¶ *After a pause, the Presiding Minister shall move the People to pray, saying,*

I COMMEND these that have been found meet to be dedicated and sent forth Missionaries, or to be set apart Deaconesses, to the prayers of the congregation.

Then shall silence be kept for a space.

¶ *Then shall follow this Prayer for Grace.*

HEARKEN, O Lord, to the prayers of thy people, and with thy never-failing protection guard them that do thee service with a devout heart, that, unhindered by any disturbance, we may ever, in our ministries, render unto thee that service which is perfect freedom; through Jesus Christ our Lord. *Amen.*

THE SENDING FORTH OF MISSIONARIES

¶ *Here they that are to be set apart Deaconnesses shall withdraw to a suitable place.*

¶ *Then shall follow a Lesson taken from the Holy Scripture.* Isaiah 6. 1-8, *or* 52. 7-10, *and* Acts 1. 8.

¶ *Then shall the Presiding Minister say to them that are to be sent forth Missionaries,*

BELOVED in the Lord, you come, for the love of God and in sincere devotion, desiring to be sent forth as Missionaries of our Lord Jesus Christ, through whom God has revealed himself in his power and grace to all mankind. You know well that to the

Church has been committed the proclamation of his Gospel, and that to chosen servants is granted this grace that they should go forth and tell abroad the message, and bring to men the gift of Christ crucified and living.

We are persuaded that you have heard this call and have pondered well to what an office and work you devote yourselves. And now, as the burden of this mission is laid upon your shoulders, we bid you to remember that the grace of God is sufficient for you in every time of need. We also bid you to have in mind how high is the privilege, and how great the joy of bringing many to the knowledge and fellowship of our Lord and Saviour.

Be assured also that, as God gives us grace, we will not cease to uphold you, for the calling is both ours and yours.

And now, that this congregation here present may know your mind and will in this thing, I ask of you,

DO you believe in one God, Father, Son, and Holy Spirit; and do you confess anew Jesus Christ as your Saviour and Lord?

Answer. I do.

DO you believe that God, in the Gospel of his love and grace, fully offers to all men forgiveness and eternal life?

Answer. I do.

DO you believe that God has called you to the office and work of a Missionary of his Gospel?

Answer. I do.

WILL you, in the strength of the Lord Jesus Christ, walk worthy of your calling, and discharge faithfully the duties of your office?

Answer. I will endeavour to do so, God helping me.

DO you promise to seek the unity and peace of the Church, and to yield yourselves to the authority of those to whom the Church has committed the direction of your work?

Answer. I do so promise, God helping me.

¶ *Then shall the Presiding Minister say,*

ALMIGHTY God bless you, and be your helper in these and all other good things. *Amen.*

¶ *Then shall the Presiding Minister say to the People,*

BRETHREN, let us now with one accord make our supplication to Almighty God on behalf of these our sisters, that he may grant them grace to fulfil their office and work.

¶ *Then shall follow this Prayer, the Candidates kneeling.*

ALL glory, praise, and thanksgiving be unto thee, O Lord our God, for that thou didst reveal thy tender love for the children of men in sending thy beloved Son for their redemption, and hast from the beginning raised up chosen servants to tell abroad the message of thy grace.

We give thee thanks that, in this company of thy messengers, thou hast numbered devoted and saintly women who have made thy Church fair with their holy work and lives, among whom we pray that thou wilt number these thy handmaidens who now present themselves before thee, and whom we, in thy name, send forth to bear the same message. Accept their love and devotion; and increase in them, we beseech thee, the gifts of thy Holy Spirit, that they may commend by teaching and example the grace of the Lord Jesus. Give them understanding, sympathy, and patience; guard them in peril of body and of soul; be thou their strength and their joy; cheer them with thy continual presence; and make them glad with the fruits of their labour.

And help us who send them forth to bear them up continually with prayer and loving thought; through Jesus Christ our Lord. *Amen.*

¶ *Then shall the Presiding Minister say to each, laying his hands upon her head,*

WE dedicate and send you forth a Missionary of Jesus Christ: In the name of the Father, and of the Son, and of the Holy Ghost. *Amen.*

¶ *And he shall deliver unto every one of them the Bible, saying,*

BE diligent to study the things which are written in this Book, that, as much as in you lieth, you may teach the Gospel of the grace of God, and be an example of faith and of holy living.

THE SETTING APART OF DEACONESSES

¶ *Then shall the Presiding Minister say,*

Let those that are to be set apart Deaconesses come forward.

¶ *Then shall a Lesson be read.* 1 Corinthians 12. 4-11.

¶ *Then shall the Presiding Minister say to them that are to be set apart,*

BELOVED in the Lord, you have read how in the beginning of the Gospel holy women ministered first to the Lord Jesus, and after his ascension to those for whom he gave his life. And you know the testimony which Saint Paul bears to the help he received in his apostolic labours from Priscilla and other helpers in the Lord, and how from age to age God has adorned his Church with the holy works and lives of devoted women.

And now, as you are minded to take upon you this service, we exhort you, in the name of the Lord Jesus Christ, that you have in remembrance to how high an office and to how weighty a charge you are called. It belongs to the Deaconess to minister to the welfare of those to whom she is sent, at home or abroad; to assist the Ministers of the Word and Sacraments in feeding and nurturing the flock; to teach the truth as it is in Jesus; to seek, advise, and pray with such as desire help in difficulties and perplexities; and to care for the sick, the poor, and needy.

As you go forth to this ministry be well assured that the Lord doth accept the services of women who love him, and who in their devotion to him tell abroad his love, comfort his people, win the careless, and lovingly bring back the wanderers to the Shepherd of their souls.

And now, that this congregation here present may know your mind and will in this thing, I ask of you,

DO you believe in one God, Father, Son, and Holy Spirit; and do you confess anew Jesus Christ as your Saviour and Lord?

Answer. I do.

DO you believe that God has called you to the office and work of a Deaconess?

Answer. I do.

WILL you, in the strength of the Lord Jesus Christ, walk worthy of your calling, and discharge faithfully the duties of your office?

Answer. I will endeavour to do so, God helping me.

DO you promise to seek the unity and peace of the Church, and to yield yourselves to the authority of those to whom the Church has committed the direction of your work?

Answer. I do so promise, God helping me.

¶ *Then shall the Presiding Minister say,*

ALMIGHTY God bless you, and be your helper in these and all other good things. *Amen.*

¶ *After this the Presiding Minister shall say to the People,*

LET us pray, dear brethren, that God in his loving kindness may pour forth his grace upon these his handmaidens, that what things they now undertake through his gracious call, they may, by his help, be enabled to fulfil.

¶ *Then shall follow this Prayer.*

IT is very meet, right and our bounden duty that we should at all times and in all places give thanks unto thee, O Holy Lord, Father Almighty, Everlasting God; but especially are we bound to praise thee, because in thy great goodness thou dost send forth labourers into thy harvest, to the increase and edifying of thy Church, and the comfort of thy people.

Graciously regard these thy handmaidens whom we, in thy name, set apart to be

Deaconesses in this Church. Send down thy Holy Spirit upon them, that they may worthily accomplish the work now committed to them; and may in all their ministrations be found faithful. Bestow upon them the gifts of wisdom and sound judgment, of simplicity and singleness of heart, and of sympathy with those among whom they dwell and work. Be thou their joy and gladness, their comfort in sorrow, their counsel in doubt, and at the last, their exceeding great reward;

Through Jesus Christ our Lord, who liveth and reigneth with thee and the Holy Spirit, ever one God, world without end. *Amen.*

¶ *Then shall the Presiding Minister lay his hands on the heads of all of them severally that are to be set apart, and he shall say,*

N. I ADMIT thee to the office and work of a Deaconess in The United Church of Canada; In the name of the Father, and of the Son, and of the Holy Spirit. *Amen.*

¶ *And he shall deliver unto every one of them the Bible, saying,*

BE diligent to study the things which are written in this Book, that, as much as in you lieth, you may teach the Gospel of the grace of God, and be an example of faith and of holy living.

¶ *Then shall the Presiding Minister proceed in the Service of the Communion or of Public Worship.*

THE SETTING APART OF DEACONESSES

¶ *And first, a Psalm or Hymn may be sung.*

¶ *Then shall be read the Gospel. St.* Mark 14. 3-9, or *St.* John 20. 11-18.

¶ *Then shall follow the Sermon.*

¶ *Before the Benediction is given, this Prayer shall be said.*

ALMIGHTY God, who art the giver of all spiritual grace and the author of everlasting life: Look with thy favour upon these thy handmaidens, and grant them grace, that they may know what things they ought to do, and have strength to do them; through Jesus Christ our Lord. *Amen.*

AN ORDER FOR

LAYING THE FOUNDATION STONE OF A CHURCH

¶ *All things being ready, the Presiding Minister with the Assisting Ministers and others shall go to the place where the Foundation Stone is to be laid; and a suitable Psalm or Hymn shall be sung.*

¶ *Then shall the Presiding Minister say to the People,*

DEARLY beloved in the Lord, we are gathered together here to lay the foundation stone of a building which we humbly trust may in due time be consecrated as a house of God.

¶ *Here may follow such a statement, suitable to the occasion, as may be desired.*

¶ *Then shall this Psalm be sung or said.*

Psalm 84.

HOW amiable are thy tabernacles, O Lord of hosts!

My soul longeth, yea, even fainteth for the courts of the Lord: my heart and my flesh crieth out for the living God.

Yea, the sparrow hath found an house, and the swallow a nest for herself, where she may lay her young, even thine altars, O Lord of hosts, my King, and my God.

Blessed are they that dwell in thy house: they will be still praising thee.

Blessed is the man whose strength is in thee; in whose heart are thy ways.

Who passing through the valley of Baca make it a well; the rain also filleth the pools.

They go from strength to strength, every one of them in Zion appeareth before God.

O Lord God of hosts, hear my prayer: give ear, O God of Jacob.

Behold, O God our shield, and look upon the face of thine anointed.

For a day in thy courts is better than a thousand.

I had rather be a doorkeeper in the house of my God, than to dwell in the tents of wickedness.

For the Lord God is a sun and shield: the Lord will give grace and glory.

No good thing will be withhold from them that walk uprightly.

O Lord of hosts, blessed is the man that trusteth in thee.

¶ *Then shall these Lessons following be read.*

1 Chonicles 29: 10-18.

WHEREFORE David blessed the Lord before all the congregation: and David said, Blessed be thou, Lord God of Israel our father, for ever and ever. Thine, O Lord, is the greatness, and the power, and the glory, and the victory, and the majesty: for all that is in the heaven and in the earth is thine;

thine is the kingdom, O Lord, and thou art exalted as head above all. Both riches and honour come of thee, and thou reignest over all; and in thine hand is power and might; and in thine hand it is to make great, and to give strength unto all. Now therefore, our God, we thank thee, and praise thy glorious name. But who am I, and what is my people, that we should be able to offer so willingly after this sort? for all things come of thee, and of thine own have we given thee. For we are strangers before thee, and sojourners, as were all our fathers: our days on the earth are as a shadow, and there is none abiding. O Lord our God, all this store that we have prepared to build thee an house for thine holy name cometh of thine hand, and is all thine own. I know also, my God, that thou triest the heart, and hast pleasure in uprightness. As for me, in the uprightness of mine heart I have willingly offered all these things: and now have I seen with joy thy people, which are present here, to offer willingly unto thee. O Lord God of Abraham, Isaac, and of Israel, our fathers, keep this for ever in the imagination of the thoughts of the heart of thy people, and prepare their heart unto thee.

Ezra 3: 10, 11.

AND when the builders laid the foundation of the temple of the Lord, they set the priests in their apparel with trumpets, and the Levites the sons of Asaph with cymbals, to praise the Lord, after the ordinance of David king of Israel. And they sang together by course in praising and giving thanks unto the Lord; because he is good, for his mercy endureth for ever toward Israel. And all the people shouted with a great shout, when they praised the Lord, because the foundation of the house of the Lord was laid.

¶ *Then shall the Minister and the People say as followeth,*

Minister. O give thanks unto the Lord, for he is gracious; for his mercy endureth for ever.

People. O give thanks unto the Lord, for he is good: for his mercy endureth for ever.

¶ *Then shall the Minister say,*

Let us pray.

O LORD God, who, although the heaven of heavens cannot contain thee, yet dost vouchsafe to dwell with thy Church here on earth: Visit, we beseech thee, with thy loving kindness, this place whereon we lay the foundation of a house to the praise and honour of thy holy name. And as thou didst fulfil the desire of thy servant David, so likewise grant that our purpose may be accomplished, that thy servants may see thy work, and their children thy glory; through Jesus Christ our Lord, who liveth and reigneth with thee and the Holy Spirit, ever one God, world without end. *Amen.*

¶ *Then shall the Minister and the People say as followeth,*

Minister. Our help is in the name of the Lord;

People. Who made heaven and earth.

Minister. Blessed be the name of the Lord;

People. From this time forth for evermore.

Minister. Behold I lay in Zion a chief corner stone, elect, precious;

People. And he that believeth in him shall not be confounded.

Minister. The stone which the builders refused;

People. Is become the headstone of the corner.

Minister. This is the Lord's doing;

People. And it is marvellous in our eyes.

Minister. Other foundation can no man lay than that is laid;

People. Which is Jesus Christ.

¶ *Then shall the Minister say,*

Let us pray.

O LORD Jesus Christ, Son of the living God, who art the brightness of the Father's glory, and the express image of his Person; the one foundation, and the chief corner stone: Bless what we now do in laying this stone in thy name, and be thou, we beseech thee, the beginning, the increase, and the consummation of this our work, which is undertaken to thy glory; who with the Father and the Holy Spirit livest and reignest, one God, world without end. *Amen.*

¶ *Then, when things are being made ready for the placing of the Stone, the Psalm following may be sung.*

Psalm 87.

HIS foundation is in the holy mountains.

The Lord loveth the gates of Zion more than all the dwellings of Jacob.

Glorious things are spoken of thee, O city of God.

And of Zion it shall be said, This and that man was born in her: and the highest himself shall establish her.

The Lord shall count, when he writeth up the people, that this man was born there.

As well the singers as the players on instruments shall be there: all my springs are in thee.

Glory be to the Father, and to the Son, and to the Holy Ghost;

As it was in the beginning, is now, and ever shall be: world without end. Amen.

¶ *Then shall the Stone be laid by the person appointed thereto, with these words.*

IN the faith of Jesus Christ, we place this Stone in this Foundation: In the name of the Father, and of the Son, and of the Holy Spirit. *Amen.*

¶ *Then shall the Minister say,*

HERE may the true faith flourish, the fear of God, the love of the brethren; in this place may the voice of prayer continually be heard, the voice of praise and the invocation of thy most holy name, even the name of the Father, and of the Son, and of the Holy Spirit; to whom be glory, henceforth and for ever. *Amen.*

¶ *Then shall the Minister say,*

Let us pray.

LET thy Holy Spirit, O Lord our God, descend continually and rest upon this place; that our gifts and all our service may be sanctified; and our hearts, and the hearts of all who labour upon this building, may be cleansed and purified; through Jesus Christ our Lord. *Amen.*

O GOD, who art the shield and defence of thy people: Be ever at hand, we beseech thee, to protect and succour the builders of this house; that the work which through thy mercy hath now been begun, may by their labour be brought to a happy end; through Jesus Christ our Lord. *Amen.*

¶ *Here may follow one or more suitable Prayers.*

OUR Father, who art in heaven, Hallowed be thy name; Thy kingdom come; Thy will be done; In earth as it is in heaven. Give us this day our daily bread. And forgive us our trespasses, As we forgive them that trespass against us. And lead us not into temptation; But deliver us from evil: For thine is the kingdom, The power, and the glory, For ever and ever. Amen.

¶ *Then shall the Hymn* Christ is made the sure foundation (*The Hymnary, No.* 163), *or other suitable Hymn, be sung.*

¶ *Here may follow Addresses and Greetings.*

¶ *Then shall the Psalm* Pray that Jerusalem may have (*The Hymnary, No.* 682), *or a suitable Hymn, be sung.*

¶ *Then shall follow the Benediction.*

AN ORDER FOR

THE DEDICATION OF A CHURCH

¶ *The Presiding Minister and those assisting him having gone to the main door of the Church, the Psalm,* Ye gates, lift up your heads (*The Hymnary, No.* 638), *or the Psalm,* All people that on earth do dwell (*The Hymnary, No.* 669), *shall be sung.*

¶ *Then, having come in through the main door, the Presiding Minister shall say,*

WE beseech thee, O Lord, graciously enter thy house, and within the hearts of thy faithful people establish for thyself an everlasting habitation, that they may be glorified by the indwelling of him by whose building they live; through Jesus Christ our Lord. *Amen.*

Peace be to this house and all that worship in it.

Peace be to those that enter and to those that go out from it.

Peace be to those that love it and that love the name of Jesus Christ our Lord.

¶ *Then shall the presiding minister and those assisting him move forward to their place; and meanwhile the Psalm,* I joyed when to the house of God (*The Hymnary No.* 682) *or a suitable Hymn, shall be sung.*

¶ *Then shall the Presiding Minister receive the keys of the Church, and shall place them on the Table.*

¶ *Then shall he say,*

Let us pray.

O LORD Jesus Christ, who openest and no man shutteth: Grant that this house, now opened for thy service, may always be filled with thy presence, and may ever remain a refuge for thy faithful people; who with the Father and the Holy Spirit livest and reignest, one God, for ever and ever. *Amen.*

O ETERNAL God, mighty in power, of majesty incomprehensible; whom the heaven of heavens cannot contain, much less the walls of temples made with hands, who yet hast been graciously pleased to promise thy special presence in whatever place two or three of thy faithful servants shall assemble in thy name, to offer up their praises and supplications unto thee: Vouchsafe, O Lord, to be present with us, who are here gathered together, with all humility and readiness of heart to consecrate this place to the honour of thy great name; separating it henceforth from all ordinary and common uses, and dedicating it entirely to thy service, for reading thy holy Word, for preaching thy mighty Gospel, for celebrating thy holy Sacraments, for offering to thy glorious Majesty the sacrifices of prayer and thanksgiving, for blessing thy people in thy name, and for all other holy ordinances; that so this house may be an habitation of thy glory, and a reflection of thine everlasting light upon all who enter to meet thy presence, and to be satisfied with thy eternal love; through Jesus Christ our Lord, who with thee and the Holy Spirit liveth and reigneth, ever one God, world without end. *Amen.*

¶ *Then shall the Presiding Minister and those assisting him read in turn these parts of the Holy Scriptures, the People reverently standing.*

1. *Concerning Prayer.*

VERILY, verily, I say unto you, Whatsoever ye shall ask the Father in my name, he will give it you. Hitherto have ye asked nothing in my name: ask, and ye shall receive, that your joy may be full.

St. John 16. 23, 24.

2. *Concerning the Word of God and the Preaching of the Gospel.*

FOR as the rain cometh down, and the snow from heaven, and returneth not thither, but watereth the earth, and maketh it bring forth and bud, that it may give seed to the sower, and bread to the eater: so shall my word be that goeth forth out of my mouth: it shall not return unto me void, but it shall accomplish that which I please, and it shall prosper in the thing whereto I sent it.

Isaiah 55. 10, 11.

I SAW another angel fly in the midst of heaven, having the everlasting gospel to preach unto them that dwell on the earth, and to every nation, and kindred, and tongue, and people. *Revelation* 14. 6.

3. *Concerning Baptism.*

JESUS came and spake unto them, saying, All power is given unto me in heaven and in earth. Go ye therefore, and teach all nations, baptizing them in the name of the Father, and of the Son, and of the Holy Ghost: Teaching them to observe all things whatsoever I have commanded you: and, lo, I am with you alway, even unto the end of the world. *St. Matthew* 28. 18-20.

4. *Concerning Confirmation.*

NOW when the apostles which were at Jerusalem heard that Samaria had received the word of God, they sent unto them Peter and John: who, when they were come down, prayed for them, that they might receive the Holy Ghost. *Acts* 8. 14, 15.

5. *Concerning Matrimony.*

FOR this cause shall a man leave his father and mother, and shall be joined unto his wife, and they two shall be one flesh. This is a great mystery: but I speak concerning Christ and the Church. *Ephesians* 5. 31, 32.

6. *Concerning the Burial of the Dead.*

I WOULD not have you to be ignorant, brethren, concerning them which are asleep, that ye sorrow not, even as others which have no hope. For if we believe that Jesus died and rose again, even so them also which sleep in Jesus will God bring with him.

1 Thessalonians 4. 13, 14.

7. *Concerning the Lord's Supper.*

I HAVE received of the Lord that which also I delivered unto you, That the Lord Jesus the same night in which he was betrayed took bread: And when he had given thanks, he brake it, and said, Take, eat: this is my body, which is broken for you: this do in remembrance of me. After the same manner also he took the cup, when he had supped, saying, This cup is the new testament in my blood: this do ye, as oft as ye drink it, in remembrance of me. For as often as ye eat this bread, and drink this cup, ye do shew the Lord's death till he come.

1 Corinthians 11. 23-26.

¶ *Here may the Hymn Veni Creator Spiritus* (*The Hymnary, No.* 143), *be sung.*

¶ *Then shall the Presiding Minister and all the People speak these words of dedication on their part.*

Minister. O God, the Father of our Lord Jesus Christ; our Father which art in heaven:

People. To thee we dedicate this house.

Minister. O God the Son; Saviour of the world; Head over all things to the Church; Prophet, priest, and king of thy people:

People. To thee we dedicate this house.

Minister. O God the Holy Spirit; Given to be our abiding teacher, sanctifier, and comforter; Lord and giver of life:

People. To thee we dedicate this house.

Minister. Holy, blessed, and glorious Trinity, three Persons and one God:

People. To thee we dedicate this house.

¶ *Here may be sung the Hymn* Only-Begotten, Word of God eternal (*The Hymnary, No.* 197).

¶ *Then shall follow this solemn Prayer, beseeching God, on his part, to consecrate the House to its holy use; the Presiding Minister standing at the Table, and saying,*

The Lord be with you;

Answer. And with thy spirit.

Minister. Lift up your hearts;

Answer. We lift them up unto the Lord.

Minister. Let us give thanks unto our Lord God;

Answer. It is meet and right so to do.

Then shall the Minister continue,

IT is very meet, right, and our bounden duty, that we should at all times and in all places, give thanks unto thee, O Holy Lord, Father Almighty, Everlasting God; for that thou, according to thy most true promise by Jesus Christ our Lord art present in our prayers and holy rites, and in all the services of these thy servants.

Let thy Holy Spirit descend with the fullness of sevenfold grace in the dedication which we, thy unworthy servants, now make; to the glory of thy holy name; in honour of thy Son, our Lord Jesus Christ, who hath vouchsafed to redeem us upon the holy Cross; and in special remembrance of his most glorious Resurrection: that, whensoever thy holy name is invoked within these walls, the prayers of all those who call upon thee may be heard by thee, O Lord, merciful and gracious.

O blessed Majesty of God, filling, containing, and ordering the whole world;

O holy King of Saints, upholder and defender of the universal Church;

O blessed Hand of God, sanctifying, blessing, and replenishing all things;

O blessed and holy Trinity, who dost give purity, strength, and beauty to that which thou hast created: We most humbly beseech thee of thy mercy that thou wouldest vouchsafe to bless, hallow, and consecrate this Table of Communion: and bless and consecrate this whole building with the everlasting fullness of thy sanctifying power; who livest and reignest, ever one God, world without end. *Amen.*

¶ *Then shall be sung the Hymn* Christ is made the sure foundation (*The Hymnary, No.* 163).

¶ *Then shall the Presiding Minister say, the People standing,*

BY virtue of our sacred office in the Church we do now declare to be consecrate, and set apart from all profane and common uses, this house of God under the name of . . . : In the name of the Father, and of the Son, and of the Holy Ghost. *Amen.*

NOW unto the King eternal, immortal, invisible, the only wise God, be honour and glory for ever and ever. *Amen.*

¶ *Then shall the Minister give a Blessing in these words.*

MAY the power and presence of God be with you in all that you do for him in this his own habitation. *Amen.*

¶ *Then shall the Presiding Minister proceed in the Service of Public Worship.*

¶ *If it be not convenient for the Presiding Minister and those assisting him to come in at the door of the Church, the Service may begin with the Psalm or Hymn preceding the delivery of the keys of the Church.*

AN ORDER FOR
THE DEDICATION OF CHURCH FURNISHINGS AND MEMORIALS

¶ *At the time appointed, the Minister, accompanied by any who may take part with him in the service, shall proceed to that part of the Church where the act of dedication is to take place; and, the People standing, he shall say one or more of the following sentences,*

OUR help is in the name of the Lord, who made heaven and earth.

Give unto the Lord, O ye kindreds of the people, give unto the Lord glory and strength.

Honour and majesty are before him: strength and beauty are in his sanctuary.

All scripture given by inspiration of God is profitable for doctrine, for reproof, for correction, for instruction in righteousness, that the man of God may be perfect, throughly furnished unto all good works.

This is the table that is before the Lord.

The cup of blessing which we bless, is it not the communion of the blood of Christ? The bread which we break, is it not the communion of the body of Christ?

Jesus said, All power is given unto me in heaven and in earth. Go ye therefore, and teach all nations, baptizing them in the name of the Father, and of the Son, and of the Holy Spirit.

Let us pray.

BLESSED and glorious Lord God Almighty, by whose power, wisdom and love all things are sanctified, enlightened and made perfect: Be merciful unto us and bless us, we beseech thee, and cause thy face to shine upon us, that what we now do may please thee, and show forth the honour of thy name. Let thy work appear unto thy servants, and thy glory unto their children. And let the beauty of the Lord our God be upon us: and establish thou the work of our hands upon us; yea, the work of our hands establish thou it; through Jesus Christ our Lord. *Amen.*

¶ *This Order of Dedication, together with the appropriate Prayer for each occasion, shall be followed.*

¶ *The Minister may call upon the Person appointed to perform the unveiling.*

WE ask N. now to unveil the memorial (*or* Gift).

The Minister may be asked, in such words as these, to receive the Memorial (or *Gift*).

REVEREND Sir,
In memory of N. (*or* in the name of N.), we ask you to receive this Memorial (*or* Gift) and to dedicate it to the glory and praise of God.

Then shall the Minister say,

WE accept this Memorial (*or* Gift) as a sacred trust, and shall treasure it with reverence and gratitude.

¶ *And he shall pronounce the words of Dedication.*

IN the faith of Jesus Christ, we dedicate this Memorial (*or* Gift): To the glory of God; (and in memory of N.); In the name of the Father, and of the Son, and of the Holy Spirit. Amen.

¶ PRAYERS

I

At the Dedication of a Window the Minister shall pray in this wise.

ALMIGHTY God, who art the true light of faithful souls and the perfect brightness of thy saints, and who fillest heaven and earth with thy divine majesty, but who dost accept the offerings of thy children: Graciously receive at our hands this Window, which we dedicate unto thee (in memory of thy servant), to the beautifying of this sanctuary, to the blessing and edifying of this thy people, and to the glory of thy great name; through Jesus Christ our Lord. *Amen.*

II

At the Dedication of a Pulpit or Lectern the Minister shall pray in this wise.

ALMIGHTY God, who dost enlighten the minds of thy servants with the knowledge of thy truth: Cause thy Church to arise and shine. Let thy blessing rest, O Lord, upon this Pulpit (*or* Lectern) which we dedicate to thee. Grant that thy truth here made known to thy worshipping people may be effectual unto their faith and eternal life. May all who read be filled with the faith of the Gospel, and with thankfulness to thee who dost in the Holy Scriptures reveal the Word of life. And grant that all who hear may receive that Word into honest and good hearts, and bring forth fruit with patience, to thy glory; through Jesus Christ our Lord. *Amen.*

III

At the Dedication of a Communion Table the Minister shall pray in this wise.

ETERNAL God, Father of our Lord Jesus Christ, of whom every family in heaven and earth is named: Accept us through him, we beseech thee, and hear us as we dedicate to thy glory this Communion Table, and pray thee, through the grace of thy Holy Spirit, to hallow and consecrate it to the holy uses for which it is set apart.

Grant that whensoever thy people come hither in obedience to their Saviour's command, they may, with humble penitence and in full assurance of thy forgiveness, render unto thee the sacrifice of thanksgiving, and, receiving the Sacrament of his body and blood, be fulfilled with thy grace and heavenly benediction, and made partakers of eternal life; in the name of Jesus Christ our Lord and Saviour. *Amen.*

IV

At the Dedication of Communion Vessels the Minister shall pray in this wise.

ALMIGHTY God, who of old didst command thy servant Moses to consecrate the vessels of the sanctuary, that thereafter they might be used for thy worship and service alone: Receive at our hands, we beseech thee, these vessels which we set apart and separate from all unhallowed, ordinary, and common uses, and dedicate entirely to the service of thy house in the Sacrament of the Holy Supper of our Lord. Accept, consecrate, and bless them, we beseech thee, that ever hereafter men may know them to be holy unto the Lord. We bless thee that he, who died upon the cross for our salvation, vouchsafes to give himself to be our spiritual life and food; and we pray that whensoever thy people, in faith, receive from these vessels the Communion of his most precious body and blood, they may be made glad by the Saviour's love, quickened by his life, and fulfilled with all heavenly grace and benediction; through Jesus Christ our Lord. *Amen.*

V

At the Dedication of a Baptismal Font the Minister shall pray in this wise.

ALMIGHTY God, our heavenly Father, without whom no word or work of ours availeth, but who dost accept the works of our hands for the service of thy Church: Hearken unto the prayers of thy servants, as we dedicate this Font to thine honour and for the praise and glory of thy name.

Accept and consecrate it, O Lord, and grant that whosoever shall come hither to be baptized with water may receive also the baptism of thy Holy Spirit, and, being received into thy Church, may ever remain in the number of thy faithful children.

Let this Font ever witness to the hearts of all who worship here of the covenant into which, through baptism, they have entered with thee, that they may renew their vows as they worship, and ever seek faithfully to fulfil them, until that day when, sign and symbol having passed away, they shall see thee face to face, and glorify thee in thine everlasting kingdom; through Jesus Christ our Lord. *Amen.*

VI

At the Dedication of other Church Furnishings the Minister shall pray in this wise.

ALMIGHTY God, our heavenly Father, without whom no word or work of ours availeth, but who dost accept the gifts of our hands for the beautifying of thy sanctuary: Bestow thy blessing upon us now as we dedicate *this Gift* to thy glory, for the use and adornment of this holy place (and in memory of thy servant). Accept *it* we pray thee, as we set *it* apart from all common and unhallowed uses, ever to be devoted to the service of thy Church and the honour of thy holy name; through Jesus Christ our Lord. *Amen.*

VII

¶ *When Gifts are dedicated, the prayer here following shall be included in the Prayer of Dedication.*

WE thank thee that thou didst put into the heart of thy servant to give of *his* substance to advance the goodly order of thy house and to beautify the place of thy sanctuary; and we pray thee to accept *his* devotion, comfort *him* with thy favour, and reward *him* for the kindness he has shown to thy house and its worship.

VIII

¶ *When Memorials are dedicated, the thanksgiving here following shall be included in the Prayer of Dedication.*

O THOU who art the Creator and Lover of all men, by whom all souls do live: We bless and praise thee for all that was pure and true, beautiful and good, in the life commemorated this day; for the example *he* has left of faith and hope and duty, and of love for thy Church; and for the hope we have, through Christ, that *he* has entered into life eternal.

¶ *Then shall the Minister go on in the Service of Public Worship.*

¶ *Any article in the Church may be dedicated in the same way; that is, after the reading of suitable sentences from Holy Scripture, the Minister shall pronounce the words of dedication, and then in prayer entreat the Lord's blessing.*

AN ORDER FOR
THE DEDICATION OF AN ORGAN

¶ *An Organ may be dedicated before the Service of Public Worship begins, or after the first Prayers. In the latter case it shall not be played in the Service until it has been dedicated.*

¶ *When the time is come the Minister may make a statement suitable to the occasion.*

¶ *Then a Psalm in prose may be sung or said (The Hymnary, No.* 724, *or No.* 745, *or No.* 746); *or else a Psalm in metre may be sung (The Hymnary, No.* 642, *or No.* 664, *or No.* 666, *or No.* 668, *or No.* 669, *or No.* 688).

¶ *Then shall the Minister say,*

Our help is in the name of the Lord, who made heaven and earth.

Blessed be the Name of the Lord, from this time forth for evermore.

Let us pray.

ETERNAL God, who hast made all thy works to show forth thy glory, and hast given wisdom and understanding to thy people to devise instruments of music for thy praise: Graciously be pleased to receive at our hands this Organ, which we now dedicate to thy service; and grant, we beseech thee, that it may adorn thy worship, and assist the praises of thy people, to the glory of thy holy name; through Jesus Christ our Lord. *Amen.*

THE DEDICATION OF AN ORGAN

¶ *Then shall the Minister say,*

IN the faith of Jesus Christ, we dedicate this Instrument of music: To the glory of God; (and in memory of . . . .); In the name of the Father, and of the Son, and of the Holy Ghost. Amen.

¶ *Then may be sung, with Organ accompaniment, this Song of praise.*

GLORY be to the Father, and to the Son, and to the Holy Ghost; As it was in the beginning, is now, and ever shall be: world without end. Amen.

Or this.

PRAISE God, from whom all blessings flow;
Praise Him, all creatures here below;
Praise Him above, ye heavenly host;
Praise Father, Son, and Holy Ghost. Amen.

¶ *Then shall the Minister say,*

Let us pray.

O GOD, holy and gracious, by whom alone thy people are sanctified: Multiply thy grace upon us thy servants, that we, consecrated to thy service, may always be enabled to offer unto thee the sacrifice of our praise, and to exalt thy holy name; and at the last be numbered among them that shall sing the new song before thy throne; through Jesus Christ our Lord. *Amen.*

¶ *Then shall the Minister go on in the Service of Public Worship.*

INDEX

INDEX

INDEX

INDEX

INDEX

THE NICENE CREED

I BELIEVE in one God the Father Almighty, Maker of heaven and earth, and of all things visible and invisible:

And in one Lord Jesus Christ, the only-begotten Son of God, begotten of His Father before all worlds, God of God, Light of Light, Very God of Very God, begotten, not made, Being of one substance with the Father, by whom all things were made: who for us men, and for our salvation, came down from heaven, and was incarnate by the Holy Ghost of the Virgin Mary, and was made man, and was crucified also for us under Pontius Pilate. He suffered and was buried, and the third day He rose again according to the Scriptures, and ascended into heaven, and sitteth on the right hand of the Father. And He shall come again with glory to judge both the quick and the dead: whose kingdom shall have no end.

And I believe in the Holy Ghost, The Lord and Giver of Life, who proceedeth from the Father and the Son, who with the Father and the Son together is worshipped and glorified, who spake by the prophets. And I believe one Holy Catholic and Apostolic Church. I acknowledge one Baptism for the remission of sins. And I look for the Resurrection of the dead, And the Life of the world to come. Amen.